"All corporates are faced with the challenge of how to create support in their workplace for those employees impacted by instances of family violence. As Lisa points out in this book, the workplace can be a safe haven for victims of family violence, making it essential for employers to have an understanding of how to support and respond. In this book, Lisa shares her personal story of survival and valuable advice for workplace leaders to use in supporting their teams in being a part of the solution to this whole of society problem."

Alison Flemming
General Manager Finance, Scentre Group

"I've never heard anyone better articulate the cause, effect and resolution of domestic violence in the workplace. Lisa's ability to communicate in an engaging manner what is going on and how to best support someone going through domestic violence has been invaluable."

Rob Caslick
Co-Founder Two Good Co

Lisa's natural storytelling ability helped to make the sometimes abstract concept of financial abuse and domestic violence real for our audience of government and business leaders. Lisa's down to earth yet professional communications style enabled her to connect with the audience while discussing a sometimes confronting topic.

Rebecca Wildermuth
Women's Legal Services QLD

Lisa was a pleasure to work with as she sought to understand where we were up to as a sector and how she could best add value for the journey we are on.

Lisa's skill is in bringing together the head and the heart. At our event she expertly built the case for action, while helping her audience form a personal connection with the issue. She inspired discussion and motivation for action. Thank you Lisa for such a valuable contribution to our work.

Lucy Weston
Project Manager-Customer Engagement, Water Division

Lisa was inspirational. Any businesses looking for a business focussed speaker sharing their story about surviving DV, don't look past Lisa!

Chris Patterson
Member of Parliament at Parliament of NSW

'Domestic Violence' as a presentation title isn't the easiest of subjects for people to hear. However, Lisa tackles the subject with a light heart, grace and emotion as she guides you through the stories and indicators that we should all be aware of. My entire team were engaged and actively participated throughout with plenty of questions. If the people in our studio are better informed because of the work Lisa does, that makes me a happy woman. Thank you Lisa and keep up the great work.

Emma Bannister
Founder & CEO, Presentation Studio

DOMESTIC VIOLENCE

CHANGING CULTURE, SAVING LIVES

A workplace guide for developing a
culture of empathy and understanding.

Lisa McAdams

Lisa McAdams

Breaking the Code of Silence Together

Lisa McAdams Pty Ltd

First published in Australia by Lisa McAdams Pty Ltd in 2018

© Copyright 2018 Lisa McAdams

The moral rights of the author have been asserted.

Cover and design layout by: Carolyn Sheltraw

ISBN: 978-0-6483185-0-7

Dedication

They say it takes a village to raise a child. Well, it takes a big village to help rebuild a life after domestic violence.

This book is dedicated to all the workers and volunteers on the front line. The ones who made the life I now have possible, and to all those who do this work on a daily basis. Those who work in shelters, legal service lawyers and support staff, court advocacy workers, charity workers, food banks, social workers, doctors, psychologists, counsellors, and to all those who donate their money, time and/or services

There will never be enough words to
truly express the gratitude in my heart.

Table of Contents

Acknowledgments xiii

Introduction. xix

About Lisa xxv

Part One — What is Domestic Violence?

Chapter 1 — Definitions of Domestic Violence 5

Chapter 2 — Elements of Abuse 31

Chapter 3 — Patterns of Abusive Behaviour 47

Part Two — Why is Domestic Violence a Workplace Issue?

Chapter 4 – Workplaces: Provide Safe Spaces 77

Chapter 5 – Impact on Your Organisation. 89

Chapter 6 – What Can Your Organisation Do? . . . 105

Part Three — Spotting the Signs and Communicating

Chapter 7 – Signs That You Are Being Abused . . . 123

Chapter 8 – Signs that a Co-worker is Being Abused. 133

Chapter 9 – Communicating with a Colleague in an Abusive Relationship 147

Chapter 10 — Final Thoughts 167

Appendix — Helplines and Key Statistics
   Australia 173
   Canada 177
   Ireland. 183

New Zealand 186
United Kingdom 188
United States 191

Further Reading and Resources 195

Index 197

Acknowledgments

Writing this book has been a passion project for me and is a culmination of years of learning and experience. I want to thank those who have shared their knowledge from their particular field; this has helped me grow and become the woman and business person I am today.

The following people have all in their own way helped me achieve what I have. So thank you to all of you.

Danielle Akayan, Katie Amin, Rob Caslick, Elise Mah Chat, Kath Creel, Cara Cochrane, Annabelle Daniel, Natalie Davidson, Ashley Donnelly, Catherine Harris, Maureen Kyne, Jacqui Lewis, Eliza McGivern, Kathryn Nicholson-Perry, Narelle Noble, Chris Patterson, Tania Price, Rachel Rodwell and Sam Trattles.

To my children for giving me a reason to live and the strength to do so. Because of you, I know how pure love looks and feels. Despite all I have been through I consider myself the luckiest woman in the world because I get to be your Mum.

Julia van Graas, you believed in me and saw the value in my work long before I did, thank you for being there with advice and guidance no matter how busy you were, I hope you know how much it is appreciated.

Lee Ussher, thank you for your generosity with your time, your wisdom and expertise.

Alison Flemming, for making laugh when life made me want to cry and for always encouraging me to be the best I can be.

Tanya Whitehouse meeting you was a turning point for me. I admire your passion and commitment to the work you do. You inspire me to bring my 'A' game every day. It is impossible to spend time with you without feeling better about myself and life.

Kate Savage Vickery for making my laugh, cry and everything in between and helping me stand in my power when all I wanted to do was hide in the shadows.

Chloe Cassidy, you are my heart and soul and the family I wish we had. Without you in it our world would be a bleak place. Thank you for your friendship and unconditional love.

Kathryn James for being my port in a storm, my rock when I need one and my safe place to land. No matter the distance or time difference you have always been there to listen and steady me. Please never underestimate the positive impact you have had on our lives. I am truly blessed to call you my friend.

Carolyn Sheltraw for the beautiful cover design and all the work you have designed for me in the last five years. For being a joy to work with and understanding my scribbles.

Melinda Hird for the portrait photography.

To my editor Elizabeth Stockton for your edits and insights.

Finally, I would like to acknowledge all those who have abused me, neglected me and treated me like I was less than human. Without you I would not be the person I am today, you pushed me to the very boundaries of my sanity.

By digging deep and working hard to heal I found a version of myself I am proud of. I now have the ability to educate others and make a real and lasting difference and for that I am truly grateful.

There is nothing stronger than a broken woman who has rebuilt herself – Hannah Gadsby

A Special Thank You to EY

For sponsoring my book launch. EY was an early adopter of not only Domestic Violence Policy but also training. EY is where my journey started; they were the first company to roll out my Domestic Violence Workplace Training. EY engaged me when I first started this business, moved my business forward and made it possible to get my message to a wider audience in a timeframe that would not have been achievable.

EY's commitment to this issue and our work together demonstrates the difference we can make when companies engage in this issue beyond creating policies. By being prepared to have open honest conversations we can make a positive impact.

Introduction

The workplace has the potential not only to change lives but to save them. As discussions around domestic violence have become more frequent and prominent, an increasing number of businesses are introducing new policies and procedures that address the issue. As a result, those whose lives are affected by domestic violence are now more likely than ever to come forward to ask for help in a culturally safe workplace.

But many workplaces and their employees do not understand the complexities of domestic violence, and more importantly, they do not know how to communicate effectively about it. This leaves managers out of their depth, and affected employees vulnerable to further stress, anxiety and disappointment.

If domestic violence policies are to be effective, the people who implement those policies must be equipped— not only with information, but with genuine empathy and understanding.

As someone who has had experience with both domestic violence and the corporate world, I understand what is needed. Based on the help I did (and didn't) receive, I provide strategies to help managers to successfully take the lead.

Throughout this book, I share personal stories (which will be distinguished from other text by bold italics) in order for you to understand what it is like to live in an abusive relationship, the challenges I faced, and others like me face when living in and leaving an abusive partner and rebuilding their lives.

I have created and facilitated my Domestic Violence Workplace Program into many companies; I have given keynotes sharing my own story, the financial implications of domestic abuse and its impact on business. I have also published many articles, both in the media and on my own website, on this subject.

This book is for those looking to understand the complexities of domestic violence and its impact: on those being victimised, on co-workers and on the business as a whole, including practical advice on recognising the signs, how to communicate, and importantly, what businesses can do to help both employees and customers.

Communication is key; it can make a difference to someone's safety. Being heard, believed and understood is vital. The conversation around domestic violence is growing, so don't wait until someone is sitting in front of you asking for help. Be equipped to deal with the situation when it arises.

It is my intention that this book will give you the insight you need to be better equipped to deal with the challenges of supporting co-workers, knowing your boundaries and helping to create an environment that makes victims feel safe to disclose and reach out for help.

There are helpline numbers and statistics in Appendix I from Australia, New Zealand, the USA, Canada, Ireland and the United Kingdom. I have not mentioned statistics in the main body of this book for the following reasons:

1. Statistics change, and I don't want to confuse the issue by including outdated statistics.

2. Statistics vary from country to country, so stating them throughout the book may become confusing.

3. Rather than making this a book of statistics I want you to engage with the common factors that underpin domestic violence so you can understand the devasting impact it had has on someone's life and how you can support them. If you have any doubts about how pervasive this issue is, I would suggest you google the statistics for your own country.

Important notes

- I have tried to keep this book as gender-neutral as possible. This is not done with the intent to minimise the fact the majority of domestic violence victims are women who are abused by men, but rather to acknowledge workplaces need to address the fact they comprise of both men and women. In keeping the language gender-neutral, my hope is men will find it easier to engage with the content, feel included and know they are an important part of the solution.

- In this book, I use the terms 'abused' and 'abuser'. Whilst I am wary of labelling the person rather than the behaviour, I do this for readability. I believe domestic violence is a behaviour, and the correct terminology would be 'the person being abused' and 'the person abusing'.

- There are times throughout the book when I use the terms 'victim' and 'survivor'. I am aware these terms can cause offence to some. This is not my intention. I do it because I want to make it clear domestic violence is about perpetrators victimising their partners, thus creating victims. Domestic violence is dangerous and can potentially end in homicide, therefore it is definitely something that is survived.

Personally, I am comfortable using the term 'victim' to describe both my marriage and my childhood, for the reasons stated above. I was victimised for nearly forty years, and for me, owning this and the description 'victim' helps me to make sense of the fact I spent a decade recovering. Importantly, it makes me proud I survived.

Being a victim and survivor of domestic violence is a big and important part of my life, and it helped shape the person I am, but it is far from all I am.

About Lisa

To give the stories I tell throughout the book some context, here is part of my backstory. I was born in the South of England in the late sixties. Where I lived was idyllic; from my bedroom window I could see the South Downs — miles of beautiful rolling hills. My house was so close to the sea that I could smell it. I was blessed to be raised there.

That was the only part of my childhood that was idyllic. Inside the walls of my home, I was subjected to abuse and torment on a daily basis from both my parents, to the point that I grew up believing I was so annoying that I deserved to be abused. I searched for the reason I was so unloved, believing if only I could learn to be less annoying, my family could learn to love me the way I loved them.

This search — for what it was about me that pushed people to be abusive and violent to me — would last nearly four decades.

Despite the abuse I was subjected to, I built a career I was proud of, working for a pharmaceutical marketing company in their finance department. It was a responsible job and I thrived on it. I liked working on the numbers, because numbers don't lie. I didn't like living in the grey — that was where the insecurities and abuse lived.

Feeling worthwhile was always a challenge for me. The abuse I had been subjected to as a child pushed me to be better, and in some ways it made me better at my job. At work I was happy. It was probably the first time in my life I felt I had worth.

In my twenties I met the man I was to marry. I saw him as my knight on a white horse, come to save me from my family. I truly thought he was my happily ever-after, and I could have the family and the life I had fantasised about since I was a small child.

Although he was abusive almost from the beginning, it was not out of the ordinary for me. Abuse was my normal. I still believed we could be happy. We bought a house. I loved that house; it was the first real home I had. Thinking back on how I felt having achieved the level of professional success it took to afford that home motivates me still. I was proud of myself, maybe for the first time in my life.

The relationship was far from ideal. Looking back, I wonder if my husband even liked me. If he did, he certainly didn't treat me that way. In 2001, after five years together, he got a job in Sydney. Living in Australia had been a dream of mine since I was a child, but I was scared because it meant giving up my career, my friends and all the support networks I had built up, along with the dream I had worked for and was about to start — doing a degree in political science at Sussex University.

I thought moving to Sydney would be a fresh start for both of us, that away from the pressure of our families we could build a new life and would be happy. At first, things were so good I truly believed the good life full of love and happiness had arrived. After six months, we returned to England to get married, which had already been booked and organised before we moved to Sydney.

What I remember most about my wedding is feeling sad. I put it down to the fact I was leaving England immediately afterwards. But looking back, I think deep down I knew I had just made a dangerous mistake.

I had a few jobs in Sydney, one of which was for State Crime Command, a job I loved; unfortunately, I couldn't take it on permanently because of my citizenship status at the time. I didn't have time to rebuild the career I had known in England, as we had only been in Sydney for a couple of years when I became pregnant with our first child. Our second followed quickly after.

As with many abusive relationships, once I was a stay-at-home mum things escalated quickly. Staying with my husband was not a safe option; I had already left five times, and each time I returned the abuse escalated. This is very common and something I discuss in this book.

When my youngest child was only one, I moved into a domestic violence shelter. This time I made it stick. It was the first time I had been to a shelter; it was a difficult decision to make, especially as I thought shelters were not for women like me.

I honestly didn't think women like me — who lived in affluent areas — could be abused, so I didn't recognise what was happening to me as abuse. What I now realise is that domestic abuse knows no boundaries, but truly understanding the reality of the abuse I had been subjected to would take a decade of digging deep in therapy, and a honest appraisal of the horrendous abuse to which I had been subjected.

In 2015 I started my business, consulting and training companies to help them understand what they can do to support employees and customers, and mitigate the cost to their culture and bottom line, based on the knowledge of years of working in corporations and government in a finance capacity, along with my lived experience and knowledge of abuse.

This book is a culmination of my expertise, plus the experience, knowledge and insights I have gained in the last three years working with companies to understand domestic violence and implement the best policies, procedures and training possible.

PART ONE

What is
Domestic Violence?

Important Note

Throughout this book, but particularly in part one, I describe some of the abuse to which I was subjected. I do this to give an understanding of what is like to be in an abusive relationship and deal with the impact of that abuse.

It is my intention that this be used as a reference to build knowledge and make communication easier. Because what we understand we can talk about more effectively and hopefully without judgement.

Some of the stories may be **TRIGGERING** to those who are or have been in an abusive relationship or subjected to child abuse. If you find the content triggers you please seek help from a mental health specialist, domestic violence specialist or call a help line – there are numbers for some countries in the back of the book.

CHAPTER ONE
Definitions of Domestic Violence

Understanding domestic violence is an important first step in supporting employees, co-workers, family and friends in abusive relationships. Abuse is isolating and confusing, and reaching out for help is terrifying. Often those in an abusive relationship will struggle to understand what is happening to them. Learning about the complexities of domestic violence means you can offer compassionate and appropriate support from the first disclosure.

Often times, even when victims do learn more about domestic abuse, it can still be overwhelming and confusing. It is hard to see what is happening from inside an abusive relationship. The person doing these terrible things is the person that the victim is supposed to be able to trust — the person who will always have their back. We do not expect those who love us to be systematically breaking us down mentally, emotionally and physically.

I remember not long after I left my abusive partner, I joined a help group called Living Beyond Abuse. It was a group run to help women leaving abusive relationships start to understand what had happened to them. One of the facilitators explained that being a domestic violence victim was like being a prisoner of war. I disagreed with this, because if I had been a prisoner of war, my partner would have worn a uniform, which would have made it clear to me he was not on my side. I would have known he was actively trying to undermine and hurt me.

But instead, he pretended to be on my side. He was playing the part of my best friend and closest confidant. I trusted him and told him everything—not knowing that in sharing my hopes, dreams and fears, I was actually supplying him with ammunition to hurt me. So, if I was like a prisoner of war, it was a prison where my abuser was dressed as someone I could trust.

In dealing with the aftermath of abuse, I was not left with a fear of strangers who may want to hurt me. Instead, I was left with the fear of being close to someone and loving them, knowing they could actively try and destroy me physically, mentally and emotionally.

This confusion makes it all the more important to understand domestic violence. Even the terminology can be confusing.

This is a list of some of the terms commonly used:

- Domestic Violence – DV
- Domestic Family Violence – DFV
- Intimate Partner Violence – IPV
- Domestic Abuse
- Family Abuse
- Domestic Family Abuse — DFA
- Partner Abuse
- Intimate Terrorism

There are differing opinions on the correct terms to use. Many people do not like including the word violence, as it makes people think of physical violence and does not explicitly include psychological, emotional, sexual, financial abuse. For some using the word 'abuse' makes it easier to comprehend that the situation is far more complex, and that it rests in issues of power and control.

Childhood domestic violence and child abuse

It is important to note the differences between childhood domestic violence and child abuse.

Child abuse is when a child is abused directly. As with domestic violence, this abuse can be any of the forms of abuse, including neglect. This is usually by family or primary caregivers. Childhood domestic violence is when a child witnesses abuse in their home, but is not directly abused by the perpetrator. However, subjecting children to witnessing domestic violence is a form of abuse.

Many children who witness childhood domestic violence will also be abused themselves.

Types of abuse

There are various forms of domestic violence, including:
- **Physical** abuse
- **Sexual** abuse
- **Emotional** or **psychological** abuse
- **Verbal** abuse
- **Financial** abuse
- **Spiritual/Cultural** abuse
- **Technologically Facilitated Abuse** — TFA
- **Image-based** abuse

When most people think of domestic violence, an image of physical violence comes to mind. I have had conversations with women who have left an abusive relationship, but because they were never physically assaulted, they felt they hadn't been subjected to 'real' domestic abuse.

This is not surprising, because the images we see in the media are mostly of a woman looking broken with an obvious black eye. That is the public face of domestic violence, but it is only a fraction of the story.

In order to shed some light on the complexities of domestic violence, here is a more detailed list of different forms of abuse, in no particular order:

- **Emotional and Psychological Abuse** – Includes humiliation, shaming and blaming.
- **Financial Abuse** – Controlling money and limiting access to finances. Not allowing financial independence. Accruing debt in the abused person's name fraudulently or through coercion.
- **Social Abuse** – Isolation from friends and family. Limiting access to phone and computers. Shutting the victim off from their support network.
- **Verbal Abuse** – Name-calling, put-downs, swearing and shouting.
- **Physical Abuse** – Threats of physical violence or actual physical violence, including punching, kicking, shoving and choking. Threatening and/

or assaulting children and pets. Throwing things, and/or breaking things.

- **Spiritual and Cultural** – Using spiritual or cultural beliefs to justify violence and force compliance. Denying the victim access to their spiritual community.
- **Sexual Abuse** – Sexual assault and abuse. If sex is not consensual, then it is sexual abuse.
- **Stalking** – Excessive contact including phone calls, social media, physically following.
- **Technologically Facilitated Abuse** – With the growth of social media, this is an emerging form of abuse. It is using social media to stalk the victim with or without their knowledge. Content uploaded or changed. Tracking devices being installed on phones, computers, smart televisions, hidden cameras and GPS devices. Even keystroke monitors may be used to track what is searched on a computer.
- **Image-Based Abuse** – This is also referred to as Revenge Porn, although there is a push to eliminate this term as it implies both that the victim has done something to make the abuser seek revenge, and that it is connected to pornography. Having someone share intimate pictures of you is harrowing and dehumanising. Using the threat of sharing these images gives the abuser control over their victim.

The descriptions above are brief, but it is easy to see that there is more to domestic violence than physical abuse alone.

Although the devastating effects of physical abuse cannot be denied, it is also true that the effects of all abuse can be equally debilitating. The confusion that a person can feel when being psychologically and emotionally abused in the absence of physical abuse can lead them to feel like they are imagining things, and that the abuse is not occurring.

People who are being abused without suffering physical abuse find it more difficult to recognise that abuse is taking place. For this reason, the abuse can escalate over time, and the person becomes slowly accustomed to being abused. There is no definitive line crossed, and lack of knowledge about the types of abuse makes it difficult to recognise.

I have been told countless times that someone's partner was controlling, but that the situation wasn't abuse because they were not hit. They then go on to describe a clearly abusive relationship.

It is important to know the forms of abuse, because whether you think you may be in an abusive relationship or know someone (a co-worker, employee, friend or family member) in an abusive relationship, the more information you have, the better-equipped you are to understand and help.

Even if you think you don't know anyone who has experienced abuse, the shame and secrecy surrounding domestic violence mean that you could know more than one person and just not realise, because they keep it hidden, or do not realise their relationship is abusive.

Physical abuse

Not many abusive relationships start with physical abuse. Usually, there is a slow eroding of the sense of self for the partner of an abuser, as will be explained in the discussions of other forms of abuse.

Physical abuse can involve any of the following violent acts:
- Punching
- Slapping
- Pushing or shoving
- Kicking
- Scratching or biting
- Choking or strangling
- Throwing things
- Using weapons or objects that could hurt you
- Physically restraining you (such as pinning you against a wall, floor, bed, etc.)
- Reckless driving
- Other acts that hurt or threaten you.
- Threatening violence against children, family members or friends or actually committing violence

against children, family members or friends
- Threatening violence against pets or actually committing violence against pets

Physical violence is not a constant in all relationships. Abuse is about power and control, and physical violence will be used to gain control back. This control can be something outside of the relationship, such as the abuser being embarrassed by a friend or co-worker. But control over their partner will address the power balance inside.

Alcohol and physical violence

There are a lot of misconceptions about physical abuse and alcohol. Many people believe that alcohol causes physical abuse. This is not the case. It can exacerbate the violence, but it is not the cause. Excessive alcohol use may be related to the underlying feeling of lack of self-worth that an abuser feels, which creates the need for power and control over their partner.

As I mentioned previously, after I left my abusive marriage I went to a support group called Living Beyond Abuse. There, someone mentioned that alcohol was the cause of the violence she had faced, and we were then told this:

The partner who had hit her drunk had managed to NOT hit anyone in the pub and NOT hit anyone on the way home, but as soon as they walked through the door, the violence began.

If alcohol really was the root cause of violence, abusers would not only be violent toward their partners.

In fact, in my case, the violence decreased when my partner was drinking because he had been partying and was feeling in control. The times when he could not go drinking were more dangerous for me.

Sexual abuse

When discussing domestic violence and Intimate Partner Violence (IPV), we need to separate rape from sexual assault.

Rape

Rape is when someone is forced to have sexual intercourse without consent. A person must consent freely and willingly to have sex in order for it to be consensual.

A person cannot give consent if they are:
- Asleep or unconscious
- Significantly intoxicated or affected by drugs
- Unable to understand what they are consenting to, due to their age or intellectual capacity

- Intimidated, coerced or threatened
- Detained or held against their will
- They submit because the person forcing them is in a position of trust and power

In a relationship, an abuser will use some of the same strategies that are used as part of physical violence, including threatening or actually harming children, family members, friends and pets. This includes claiming that they are jealous of a child when they are not given sex on demand. They may even insinuate the child is the problem and punish the child.

Sexual assault

This includes unwanted touching, grabbing and kissing. This is often done as a show of dominance to display their power and control.

It sends a clear message of ownership. The person being abused does not have, nor are they entitled to have, bodily autonomy. They are being shown that they belong to their partner.

This sort of abuse often happens subtly in front of the abused person's children, family, friends and even co-workers. This is done to both humiliate and show dominance.

I can tell you from experience that this is completely dehumanising, especially when done in front of co-workers. It is debilitating to be in front of your peers whom you respect and be treated in such a demeaning way.

Reproductive abuse

This is where a person is subjected to control over their right to choose when it comes to the decision to have a baby. This can be either by restricting access to birth control, being forced into unprotected sex or being coerced into keeping the baby when pregnant. This is often done because having a baby limits women's independence and earning capacity, making them even more dependent on their abusers.

The other side of this is being coerced or forced into having an unwanted abortion. Some abusers find the thought of sharing their partner with a baby overwhelming and will do anything to prevent this.

Emotional and psychological abuse

I am finding it difficult to even start writing about psychological abuse, even now, over a decade since I left my abusive relationship. The effects of this abuse on my psyche make this section challenging to write. When you are in a relationship that is emotionally abusive, it is so difficult to comprehend what is happening to you.

I feel an intense desire to get this right, so that it is easier for you to understand how it feels to be in the grips of emotional abuse.

One of the important things to understand is when someone is in an abusive relationship, they do not see the way their partner treats them as abusive. This confusion leads to self-blame — not only for the problems in the relationship, but for all the abusive partner's behaviour.

Abusers will use any means necessary to gain control of their partners, including:

- **Intimidation** – They will use threats, such as saying they will leave or hurt you or loved ones. *In my relationship, he would use many forms of intimidation, including threatening to tell intimate secrets to co-workers.*
- **Bullying** – This looks like any other form of bullying and is just as damaging. *This would include name-calling and explaining that I was annoying, not only to him, but to everyone else too.*
- **Isolation** – This takes many forms, from moving house to restricting access to friends, family and co-workers, etc. *In my case, he would make me feel guilty, or he would block my calls so I didn't receive invites.*

- **Humiliating and shaming** – This is soul-destroying, especially from someone you love. *Because I came from an abusive childhood, my ex would use that to prove that everything was my fault. He would tell me, 'Even your own parents can't stand you.' When I called him out on it, he would say, 'I just want you to stand up to them. Maybe I love you too much, but I hate what they do to you.' It was so confusing.*
- **Threatening and coercing** – These are not necessarily physical threats. Abusers threaten to reveal secrets, leave, withhold affection or money, and really make any threat they can think of. The more the abuser gets to know their partner, the better they get at this.
- **Belittling** – Abusers will belittle everything, from how the abused holds a fork, to how they stand or even how they watch the television. Often, these comments are said 'with love', so it erodes the victim's sense of self-worth.
- **Emotionally cold and distant** – This is very isolating and will often leave the abused partner craving affection from their abuser.

Verbal abuse

Being insulted, called names and put down are difficult if they happen once or twice. But in an abusive relationship, they happen over and over.

Every little thing you do or say is open to attack. It is exhausting. When the person verbally abusing you is your partner, they have intimate knowledge of you, meaning they know exactly how to hurt you and what to say for maximum impact.

> *I had a therapist who called this 'precision point abuse'.*
>
> *My ex-partner used to say to me all the time, 'Everybody thinks you're boring. You get on everybody's nerves.'*
>
> *I didn't realise at the time, but every time he said the word 'everybody' it implanted itself into my psyche. It eroded my confidence until I hated going out and being around people, because I hated the thought of boring people. Making new friends became almost impossible. I doubted myself and whether I was worthy of friends.*
>
> *The insults and put-downs were normal. I became very self-critical, to the point that I would verbally abuse myself.*

Verbal abuse is very difficult to recover from, because the terrible things you have been called become your 'new normal' way of thinking. It takes a great deal of practice to change those negative tapes in your head.

For me, the more often I heard positives about myself and that I didn't deserve to be spoken to like that, the better I started to feel about myself.

It is important to know and remember, challenging an abuser on their behaviour in front of their partner or in their partner's absence can put the abused in danger. Abusers do not like to be challenged, so if you are going to speak up, be sure it is the best interest of the abused.

Financial abuse

When I discuss the other forms of abuse I was subjected to, they are in the past. I am no longer physically, sexually, psychologically or verbally abused in my daily life. I have spent years healing from this. Although it can be triggering to discuss these other forms of abuse, they no longer affect me directly.

I cannot say the same for financial abuse, as this takes a long time to rebuild from and is the reason I am so passionate about doing all I can to ensure the financial security of others.

Pull back the curtain on my life, and you will see that I am still impacted by financial abuse to which I was subjected. I left my abusive marriage with two bags of clothes, one bag of toys, $33.00 in my purse and thousands of dollars in debt.

It was over a decade ago so I was fortunate my bank understood the devastating effect domestic violence had on my financial situation. They helped me by reducing my debt and giving a repayment plan I could afford. Without this understanding and assistance I would have been forced into bankruptcy. As a business owner I am acutely aware of the negative this would have had on my future, and continue to feel gratitude for the person at the bank who helped me.

This enabled me to create opportunities and I have worked hard, but the climb out of poverty is not an easy one. My children's long-term financial future is the source of my personal motivation.

Debt caused by financial abuse is often referred to as 'sexually transmitted debt,' which is an expression I personally loathe. There are too many connotations about sexually transmitted diseases being the fault of women, who are perceived in a negative light due to their sexual activity. I do not hold with this view, but that doesn't mean it does not exist, which is why I find this term at best unhelpful.

Financial abuse increases the dynamic of dependence between an abuser and their partner. The partner often has:
- No access to money
- No control over finances
- Responsibility for any debt
- Responsibility for bills but no access to funds, meaning that all their money goes towards basics like food and other essentials, and the abused are forced to take out loans, or increase credit card debt.
- Total control of the finances however with not enough money to cover everything, often pushing the abused into debt.

In my own relationship, I became completely dependent on my partner. I had no access to money, and therefore I could see no way out. I felt trapped in this never-ending cycle of poverty and abuse. But to the outside world, it looked like I had it all. It was a lie. It was all smoke and mirrors.

Even today, I often receive no child support, so I must financially support my children alone. I was often left with the choice between investing in my business in order for it to grow, or meeting my children's needs. Even with my level of understanding about the dynamics of abuse, I still occasionally felt a paralysing sense of shame.

When I met my ex-partner, I had savings. I actually paid off his debts and did the paperwork for county court judgements he had, due to bad debt. To be left with less than nothing was devastating. The sense of perceived failure stayed with me for a long time.

The impact of financial abuse is far-reaching and can take decades to overcome. This is why it is so important for businesses to ensure their staff are trained and to create an environment where employees feel safe to reach out for help (and know who to reach out to).

Technologically facilitated abuse

It is easier to be stalked and monitored than is was a decade ago.

> *Since I left my abusive partner the world has changed a great deal. The advent of social media has made it much easier for perpetrators to both stalk and intimidate their victims. Advances in technology have increased the potential to be tracked and monitored. This makes it more dangerous and difficult to escape abusive relationships and remain safe; with easy access to tracking and monitoring devices the abuser can easily track and locate their partner.*
>
> *In the mid 2000s, when I left, I only had to worry about my emails being hacked and a constant barrage of text messages. That was intimidating enough, and could leave me confused and paralysed with fear. I can only imagine the depth of fear and intimidation someone would feel today.*

Today it is a whole new ball game. The technological advances made in the last decade have been amazing and ground-breaking. As a business owner, these tools have been incredibly positive. But they have also equipped abusers with new weapons of power and control — the two things that are vital for abusers to maintain their abusive hold on the abused.

A lot of people use the same password for everything, and often people know their partner's passwords, which makes the abused very vulnerable to hacking from the abuser.

There are four main elements to technologically facilitated abuse:

1. **Harassment** – The abuser will use social media, email, SMS and other tools to harass the victim. This enables them to stay in their victim's life and keep control over them. This harassment instils fear, which also helps the abuser to retain control.

2. **Monitoring and stalking** – With today's technology, it is easy for the abuser to monitor and stalk. There are so many tracking devices available. A smart television can be set up to watch and listen to everything. Tracking devices can be put in phones, strollers, toys, bags or cars. Any place where you can hide a small object, you can put a tracking device. With GPS on our phones, our own smartphones effectively function as tracking devices. With apps available designed specifically to find friends or locate lost phones, this is easily done and makes the abused person vulnerable.

3. **Impersonation** – This comes in two forms:
   - The abuser will impersonate someone the abused knows to gain access to the abused partner's social media accounts. This means the abused is unaware that the abuser has access to their LinkedIn, Facebook, Twitter, Instagram or Snap Chat accounts. If location settings are enabled, the abuser can build a good picture of their movement without the need for tracking devices.
   - The abuser may use their knowledge to impersonate the abused on social media, usually without the abused partner's knowledge. The abuser will use this to make the abused look bad, hurting friendships and professional relationships. This is another tool to isolate the abused, by causing friction with friends, family and co-workers.

4. **Threats/Punishment** – The abuser will have 24-hour access to their partner or ex-partner through social media to threaten and punish the abused. This can range from threatening the abused partner, their children, their family or even their pets. Abusers may often threaten to spread lies to the abused partners' co-workers, which can make them fear for their job. This keeps the power and control firmly in the hands of the abuser.

When the abused leaves, the abuser's power and control is disrupted. The abuser will do what it takes to gain back control, which leaves both the abused person and the company they work for vulnerable to breeches in cyber security and cyber hacking as the abuser uses technologically-facilitated abuse to gain back their control by whatever means possible.

Companies need to help employees in this situation to keep their virtual presence secure. Employees are privy to a great deal of confidential and sensitive material about the companies they work for, so helping them deal with technologically facilitated abuse makes sense both ethically and economically.

There are steps that organisations can take to secure their data and support their employees once they know that domestic violence poses a potential threat. The focus of this book is not about the technicalities of cyber security, but these steps could include:

- Changing passwords on a daily basis.
- Limiting access to sensitive files on any laptop that may be taken home.
- Encouraging use of work phone to make work calls.
- Sweeping work devices for potential bugs and GPS that have been added

Spiritual and Cultural Abuse

In my culture divorce is accepted as a cultural norm. There was no stigma for me to leave and become a divorcee. This is not the case for all cultures. I know someone who is in a dangerous and violent relationship, but leaving her husband is not an option.

If she left, her own family would disown her and she would certainly lose access to her support network and most importantly her child. Despite being the main bread winner in the family she chooses to stay for the sake of her child. I am lucky to be in a position where I do not have to make these decisions.

It is important we understand a person from their reality not ours, if we are to offer true empathy and understanding.

It is important to understand the LGTBI community and how domestic violence effects couples in that community.

The first thing I needed to understand was the terminology because if I was to understand the impact of DV in this community I needed a better understanding of the community itself. Starting with the terminology, although this is not a definitive list, it is one of the most commonly used:

L Lesbian **G** Gay **B** Bisexual **T** Transgender **I** Intersexed **Q** Queer

Let's start with the similarities; power and control is at the root of DV and this is no different in this community. Although there is limited data, LGBTIQ people are as likely as non-LGBTIQ people to be victims of DV. The impacts of domestic and family violence and trauma are equitable as is the fear that you won't be believed. Victim blaming or self-blaming is a debilitating element of DV that is universal.

The differences for lesbian, gay and bisexual people is using someone's sexuality against them, threatening to "out" someone, or cutting them off from community events. The transgender, intersex and gender diverse may be subjected to their partners threatening to "out" their gender history.

They will be subjected to partner's using offensive pronouns such as "it", ridiculing their partner's body/appearance/identity, telling their partner that he or she is not a "real" man or woman. Imagine the effect it must have when you already have to deal with society's judgement of who you are as a person.

Diversity and Inclusiveness needs to be a factor in domestic violence awareness programs and policy creation and this needs to extend to LGBTIQ, culturally diverse, and indigenous employees. A company that fosters a diverse, inclusive and supportive work environment will have a positive impact on not only individuals but company culture as a whole.

CHAPTER TWO
Elements of Abuse

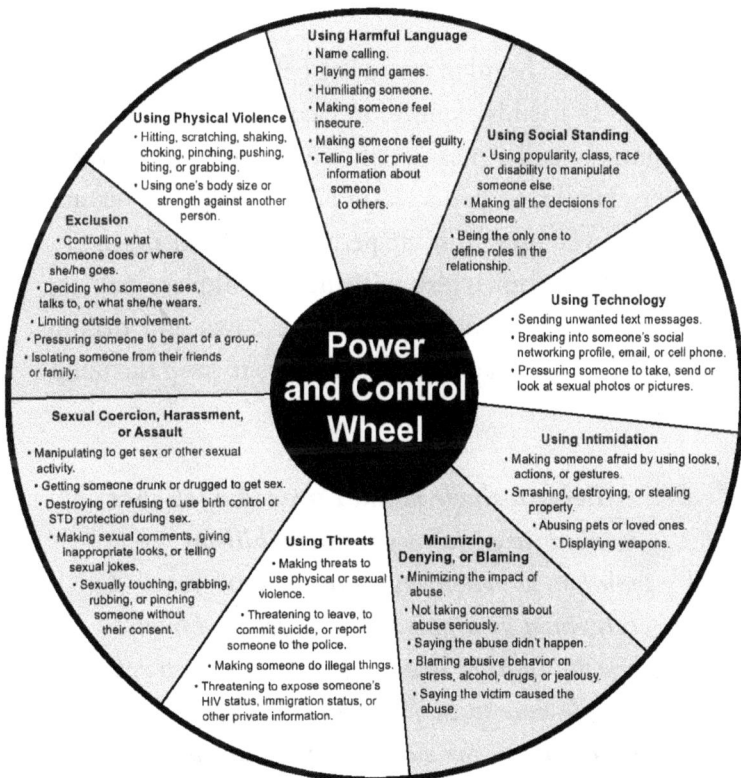

Power and Control Wheel

Using Harmful Language
- Name calling.
- Playing mind games.
- Humiliating someone.
- Making someone feel insecure.
- Making someone feel guilty.
- Telling lies or private information about someone to others.

Using Social Standing
- Using popularity, class, race or disability to manipulate someone else.
- Making all the decisions for someone.
- Being the only one to define roles in the relationship.

Using Physical Violence
- Hitting, scratching, shaking, choking, pinching, pushing, biting, or grabbing.
- Using one's body size or strength against another person.

Exclusion
- Controlling what someone does or where she/he goes.
- Deciding who someone sees, talks to, or what she/he wears.
- Limiting outside involvement.
- Pressuring someone to be part of a group.
- Isolating someone from their friends or family.

Using Technology
- Sending unwanted text messages.
- Breaking into someone's social networking profile, email, or cell phone.
- Pressuring someone to take, send or look at sexual photos or pictures.

Sexual Coercion, Harassment, or Assault
- Manipulating to get sex or other sexual activity.
- Getting someone drunk or drugged to get sex.
- Destroying or refusing to use birth control or STD protection during sex.
- Making sexual comments, giving inappropriate looks, or telling sexual jokes.
- Sexually touching, grabbing, rubbing, or pinching someone without their consent.

Using Intimidation
- Making someone afraid by using looks, actions, or gestures.
- Smashing, destroying, or stealing property.
- Abusing pets or loved ones.
- Displaying weapons.

Using Threats
- Making threats to use physical or sexual violence.
- Threatening to leave, to commit suicide, or report someone to the police.
- Making someone do illegal things.
- Threatening to expose someone's HIV status, immigration status, or other private information.

Minimizing, Denying, or Blaming
- Minimizing the impact of abuse.
- Not taking concerns about abuse seriously.
- Saying the abuse didn't happen.
- Blaming abusive behavior on stress, alcohol, drugs, or jealousy.
- Saying the victim caused the abuse.

Wheel Developed by: Domestic Abuse Project, Duluth, MN

It is essential to understand the behaviours that make it possible for someone to abuse and control their partner and keep them trapped in an abusive relationship, as shown in the power and control wheel above. Knowing how these controlling and coercive behaviours work will help you to understand how someone gets trapped in an abusive relationship and why they don't 'just leave'.

Grooming

I had not even heard of grooming before I left my abusive partner. If friends, family and co-workers understood grooming—and I mean really understood it—then our society would be better equipped to help victims and possibly even prevent some perpetrators from abusing.

This behaviour is also relevant to workplace bullying and harassment. Breaking someone down and making them feel inadequate and fearful helps to keep the bullying secret.

> *Being a single mum, I needed a job that worked around my responsibilities as a mother, so when my children were young I retrained as a personal trainer and health coach. In this area my job was to teach people how to be fitter and healthier — to groom them for success. There are various*

techniques a coach can use to change some-one's thinking and behaviours.

My job was to create more positive thoughts and improve self-esteem and self-worth. I worked to empower my clients to take better care of themselves and to use the healthy skills I had taught them.

Coaching — whether it be health, sport, business or any other form — is effectively positive grooming.

In an abusive relationship, grooming starts as soon as the abuser meets a potential partner, and works similarly to coaching, but instead of creating a positive outcome, the abuser is undermining their partner — slowly eroding their partner's confidence, self-esteem and self-worth and creating a dependence of the abused to their abuser.

This grooming is done so subtly that it is hardly notice-able as abuse. It creates a feeling of unease in the partner, which is reflected back on them as being untrusting or needy. Through grooming the abused partner starts to lack confidence; the abuser can start to gain control. Slowly, the abused partner accepts a lower standard of treatment, and abuse is the new normal. Over time, the abusive behaviour feels like the way things have always been.

Growing up in a loving home does not make someone immune to an abusive relationship, but it will mean the grooming process will take longer — sometimes years.

Maybe the entrapment phase will last until after marriage or until pregnancy. Remember, nobody is immune to domestic violence.

Some abused partners will have been groomed over several relationships or even from childhood to think that abusive behaviours are normal. I call this pre-groomed.

Pre-groomed

> *My ex-partner first hit me one month into our relationship. People are often surprised and comment, 'Really? After only a month? That's quick.'*
>
> *To understand why I took this behaviour as normal, you need to understand the long-term effect being abused as a child had on my sense of what was normal. As stated above, I was pre-groomed. Abuse was my normal.*
>
> *A lifetime of abuse meant I accepted being punched by my partner after only one month of grooming by him, because I had already been taught to accept that I was not worth much and that, if I was hit, it was my fault.*
>
> *I was in my twenties when I met him. I had been abused since I was born.*

Effectively, I had been groomed for over two decades. I had already made some pretty bad choices when it came to men. It really didn't take much work for me to accept that it was my fault that he had hit me. To the point, I felt guilty for driving him to hit me and making him feel bad.

If I had had a nice childhood, it would've probably taken my ex many months or even years to groom me, by subtly putting me down to get me to accept that it was my fault that he hit me. But in my case, this work had already been done for him.

Crazy-making

For me, the crazy-making began slowly. Here is one instance that started when we had not been together for long:

I got back in the car after filling it with petrol. He looked at me with complete adulation; being looked at like that is the most amazing feeling you can imagine. It was like I was his everything. I had longed to be adored like that since I could remember.

I asked him, "Why are you looking at me like that?"

He replied, smiling, his eyes overflowing with love, *"I just admire you so much, you are amazing."*

I was surprised. *"What did I do that is so amazing? I only got petrol."*

"You just don't care what anyone thinks about you. I would get nervous, but not you."

"I don't get what you mean. I was only getting petrol. What was there to be nervous about?" I asked, confused.

"Well, I have never known anyone who puts petrol in a car so slowly. I could see that everyone waiting was getting really irritated with you. It made me feel really uncomfortable, but not you. You are so confident. You didn't even notice how angry and irritated everybody was with you!".

"Oh, I didn't realise I was slow," I said, feeling very self-conscious.

"I know. That is what I love about you."

I didn't question his sincerity, because he had said it with such love and pride. But looking back I can see why the exchange made me feel uncomfortable. On a gut-level, I knew something was off, but I didn't question it. Why would I? This was the man who loved me more than anyone. He wouldn't want me to lose confidence, surely?

The exchange ended there. I was still basking in the 'love' he was showering on me. Yet, at the same time, I felt bad, and I started the internal questioning. 'Did I get petrol slowly? Was I irritating? How could I put petrol in faster? Maybe if next time I go somewhere really quiet I can practice.'

I was losing confidence in my ability to do something I had never questioned. The next time I went for petrol, I felt shaky, and I kept looking at the other drivers for signs that I was irritating them.

Over time, I started to have an overwhelming fear of getting petrol. It was becoming almost impossible for me. I talked to my ex. He held me, kissed my head and said, "I can't stand to see you so upset. I will get the petrol for you, so don't you worry about it."

So, he did, and it slowly became something I was incapable of doing. I felt like he was my hero for saving me from the fear of getting petrol. In fact, he was the one who had created the fear.

His attitude of love and care soon turned to one of rage at my 'complete incompetence at absolutely everything'.

Years later, we were living a long way from any support network I had built up. I was alone most of the time with two babies. He would travel a lot, but he didn't have to worry about me going out and being with my friends while he was away. All he had to do was leave the car on empty, and he could trust my fear to keep me at home.

I still shudder even after a decade remembering his tyrannical rage when I told him proudly, "I did it. I filled the car with petrol. I won't have to be dependent on you to do it."

I honestly thought he would be proud of me. After all, he had been shouting at me for years about how annoying it was that 'I was so useless', but at the time, I didn't realise that he depended on my helplessness to control me. I thought he wanted what was best for me, but he wanted to control me. He would undermine me and then turn around and save me.

This is just one example. It took years to go from his first comment about my getting petrol to my complete dependence, but he was patient. There were many other ways he used this tactic. Once I had left and had some space to think, I could see the ways he used crazy-making to undermine me, but when you're in it, it is almost impossible to see the wood for the trees.

Learned helplessness

Learned helplessness could also be considered learned dependency. This is all about gaining and keeping control over a partner. Creating an inability to cope in a partner leaves the abuser with power and control over them.

> *My earlier story about getting petrol is a good example of learned helplessness. I had been taught to be dependent on my partner to put petrol in the car. Prior to being with him, I was more than capable of getting my own petrol.*
>
> *I was both helpless and dependent on my partner. This added to my sense of shame because now I was a burden. Whilst I was in the relationship, I never imagined that this was his plan. I felt bad for him that I was so 'useless' and that he had to deal with all my insecurities.*
>
> *I also felt ashamed that I was incapable of doing something so basic. I now have a better understanding of both abuse and anxiety, and whilst I am happy to be independent and capable of getting my own petrol, I see no shame in those who struggle with things and need help and support due to anxiety.*

My shame was enforced by his irritation and lack of kindness.

Gaslighting

This term comes from a film released during the 1940s, called *Gaslight*, which is about a husband who convinces his wife that she is going mad by — amongst other things — dimming the gas lights and then denying that anything is happening. Eventually, the wife becomes unable to trust her own judgement and believes, with her husband's constant reinforcement, that she is indeed losing her mind.

Gaslighting is a tactic whereby an abuser makes a victim question their reality in order to gain more power. It works more efficiently than you may think. Anyone is susceptible to gaslighting, and it is a common technique of abusers. It is done slowly, so the victim doesn't realise how much they've been indoctrinated into believing the reality set up by their abuser.

In my own abusive relationship, my partner would constantly tell me I had said or done things or that he hadn't said or done things, so that I would doubt my own perception.

Isolation

Isolation can take different forms:
- Isolating the abused from friends and/or family
- Restricting the abused partner's access to internet, social media and phones
- Moving the abused away from support networks

Isolating the abused from friends and/or family

These things can be done overtly or covertly. Sometimes the abusive partner will use gaslighting and crazy-making to make the partner believe their family and friends are the problem. This helps ensure that the abused partner breaks off contact with their support network, and enables the abuser to pretend to be concerned. It leaves the abusive partner in the powerful position of filling the void left by family and friends. Also they can threaten to disclose that the abused partner has told them something about family or friends. This can leave the abused partner feeling they will lose the love and trust of their friends or family.

This can also be done by restricting access to a car, and/or moving to a location that makes travelling by public transport difficult. Financially restricting access to money can also isolate someone.

I would often turn down invites for coffee, movies etc. due to my lack of access to money. But, as there was the perception of my having lots of money, I would lose new friendships as people saw it as a lack of interest.

Restricting access to internet, social media and phones

Again, this can be done openly by simply refusing to allow the abused partner to have access to phones and computers. Often, though, this is done covertly, such as by:

- Blocking friends and family members numbers, so the abused doesn't receive texts
- Forwarding all calls and texts to the abuser's own phone, so they are the ones responding
- Not paying bills so phones are cut off
- The abuser taking phones and computers with them when they go out

Moving their partner away from support networks

Every time I built a support network, we moved. We moved from England to Australia, which meant that I had no support at all. The only people we knew in Australia were his friends, who believed his version of me and our relationship.

When I found a strong supportive network in my mothers' group, he did not like it. In fact, it made him very angry. At the time this surprised me, because he had always said what a burden I was because I had no friends.

It was only four months after joining my mothers' group that we moved away. It was devastating. I remained close with a couple of the women from the group, but it was not the same as having them around the corner. This isolation so soon after having a baby had a detrimental effect on my wellbeing.

Victim-blaming and denial

One of the ways abusers exert power over those they abuse is by twisting the truth and blaming their victim for the abuse. From the outside, victim-blaming is hard to understand.

I commonly hear people say, 'If anybody treated me like that, I would tell them exactly what I think of the behaviour. I would not put up with it. I have too much respect for myself.' When I hear comments like this, it makes me sad at the lack of understanding that still exists around the dynamics of abuse.

When I was in my late teens, my brother (who was by then an adult) used to beat me. Sometimes it was because I had annoyed him, and other times it was because life had annoyed him. The outcome for me was the same. Neither scenario gave him the right to abuse me.

I remember after a particularly brutal beating I was told it would be best if I stayed at home so that nobody saw my injuries. The following conversation is how it was turned on me, and how it was my fault he became violent.

Me: Why should I stay home to cover your back? It is not me who beat you up.

Him: Look, I get that beating women is wrong, even my sister. But I have talked to all our friends, and they agree that if they had you as a sister, they would beat the crap out of you too. They feel bad you pushed me into hitting you. Actually, they are really angry at you.

Me: But, why would they be angry at me?

Him: Because you're not a nice person. You push people to breaking point. And now I feel like shit. I suppose you are feeling superior now?

Me: No, I didn't mean to upset you, and I don't want you to hate yourself.

Him: Yes, you did, but it backfired because now everyone hates you.

This may seem extreme, but it was a pretty normal exchange. The blame was squarely put on my shoulders, as if I could have somehow done something to control his anger and as if I should feel guilty because I didn't. I became ashamed to face people, as if I really was somehow defective. Of course, none of our friends said they thought I deserved to be beaten, but I did not know that at the time.

Getting to this stage takes time and grooming, but to me that conversation made sense. I felt bad for pushing my brother into doing something he hated himself for.

I even felt selfish for being so anxious to see our friends, when I had made him do something so dreadful. I thought about how much they must've hated me, and I wanted to hide away. That was my perception then, but not now.

Anyone who has ever been bullied will understand how it changes your perception of reality. As the bullies blame you for the abuse, it becomes the new normal. It is common to hear those who have been bullied say, 'I must have done something to deserve this, or they wouldn't pick on me'.

Add to this the trauma of others blaming the victim. I see it all the time. A victim defends their partner after the most despicable abuse, and people get annoyed with the abused, not the abuser. This perpetuates, over and over, the victim is to blame.

CHAPTER THREE
Patterns of Abusive Behaviour

Patterns of Abusive Behaviour

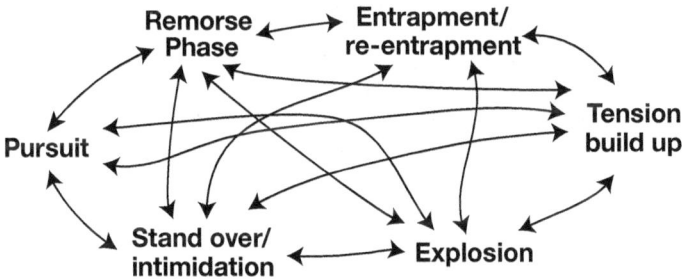

In starting this chapter, I feel it is important to state that perspectives are changing around what has been known as the 'cycle of violence'. This chapter is based on my personal and professional opinion.

For me, when I first left, I found it helpful to think of it as a cycle, although it is important to realise that each step in the cycle is abusive, whether it be covert or overt.

I no longer see this as a cycle of violence, but rather as a pattern of abusive behaviours. I now find the term 'cycle' unhelpful, because abuse does not follow a neat cycle, and can go from entrapment straight to explosion.

The below graphic depicts the long-established view of the cycle of violence. I think it is helpful to add it here because if you are supporting someone dealing with domestic violence, you will more than likely come across a graphic like this.

Cycle of Violence

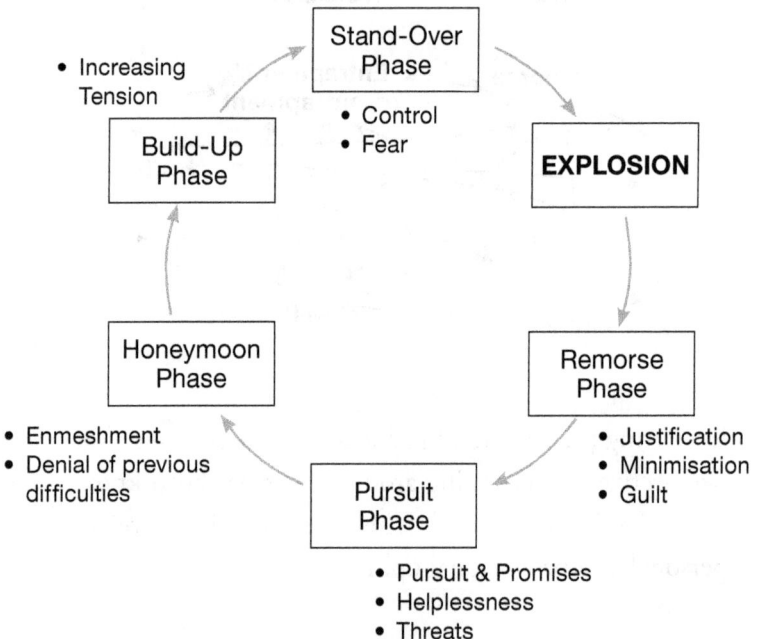

- Increasing Tension

Stand-Over Phase
- Control
- Fear

EXPLOSION

Build-Up Phase

Honeymoon Phase

- Enmeshment
- Denial of previous difficulties

Remorse Phase
- Justification
- Minimisation
- Guilt

Pursuit Phase
- Pursuit & Promises
- Helplessness
- Threats

In my own life, I first came across the concept of the cycle of violence when I entered the shelter; my crisis worker showed me the graphic. I found it comforting that I had not imagined the behaviours I had been subjected to, because life is very disorientating and confusing on the inside of an abusive relationship. It is hard to grapple with what is real and what is a distortion of the truth. As incredible as it seems to me now, I was actually unsure if what I was being subjected to constituted abuse.

The mental torture he inflicted on me for over a decade made it difficult to hold onto a thought or memory. I found it difficult to trust my own thought processes.

About a year before I left, I started writing notes to myself in a small diary that I kept hidden. They would be short notes, but enough to remind me of the things that had been said and done to me.

These are some of the things that he said to me that I found in the diaries:

'You are a freak, insane, completely unlikeable.'
'You are ugly, inside and out.'
'You are pathetic.'

'You are a vile piece of shit.'

And some other things, too hurtful and revolting to repeat.

I also diarised the abusive and intimidating way he treated me; these are direct quotes from that diary:

    'Being vile'

    'Still being vile' – four days later.

    'Out drinking, didn't come home.'

    'Bullying me today.'

    'Physical assaults started again.'

It was through these notes I first noticed there was a pattern to these behaviours. In-between, I would write things like:

    'Out to dinner.'

    'Flowers.'

    'Cooked me a meal.'

It stopped me seeing each time it reached the explosion stage in isolation, and I realised that even the times he appeared nice and behaved as though I were in charge, and he would change, it was merely an illusion. I had no control over the situation at all. Recognising this pattern ultimately helped me to break through this illusion he would change, which led me to find the strength and courage to leave.

I am reminded of this when I see my cat playing with a bug she has caught. She teases the bug, plays with it and even makes it seem like there is a chance of escape. But my cat is always in charge of the situation. She is merely toying with the bug. I felt many times like a bug, just being messed with because it was fun.

One of the common misconceptions about domestic violence is that there is constant aggression. This is rarely the case. As the diagram above shows, there is a pattern of behaviour when it comes to domestic violence. All stages are abusive and affect the abused person's psychological wellbeing and keep them engaged in the relationship. The most destructive part of this pattern is that it is almost impossible to see it when you are in it.

As I mentioned before, domestic violence is compared to being in a prison of war camp, and in a lot of ways it is. However, the big difference is that in a POW camp, you know the person is imprisoning you because of the bars, and you know that they are not on your side because they wear a uniform that identifies them as your enemy. There are no such indicators when you are in an abusive relationship.

In fact, the abuser is supposed to be on your side; you are on the same team, so it is hard to work out what is happening, and the more craziness you are subjected to, the more confusing it becomes. If you are in an abusive relationship that does not include physical violence, it can become almost impossible to work out what is going on.

An important part of recognising that a person is being abused is to recognise the patterns of behaviour.

Looking at these patterns of behaviour helps to describe the evolution of abusive relationships and the stages they typically go through, although the amount of time for each phase varies between relationships. Stages may be missed and may not occur in the order presented. Recognising the patterns of abusive behaviours in relationships can help victims and their friends, family and co-workers to understand and identify what is happening. Knowing these stages enables people to see abuse for what it is, and to relate to the differing reactions from those in the relationship.

This information can be particularly helpful in abusive relationship that do not include physical abuse. The covert and coercive nature of these patterns of behaviour can help to highlight abuse that may otherwise be explained away as part of the relationship, or worse, the victim overreacting.

Entrapment/re-entrapment phase

This is the phase that, on the surface, makes the abusive relationship seem enviably good. In reality, it is during this stage that the abused person becomes enmeshed in the relationship.

In the beginning of a relationship this phase can last days, weeks, months or even years. It can even last until after the couple is married or living together. Sadly, pregnancy is a particularly vulnerable time for women in abusive relationships, and abuse often starts or escalates during pregnancy.

As the word entrapment would suggest, it is a time when the abuser uses romance and pretend love and care, and the abused person feels everything is great. In re-entrapment the abused person starts to forget previous behaviours, as open communication appears to be happening. The abused feels heard and understood, and the entrapment has begun. These 'positive' and seemingly loving behaviours are confusing and enable the abuser to re-entrap their partner by creating the illusion of a loving and supportive relationship.

> *When I left my ex for the third time, I moved into a friend's spare room. It was a stressful time. My ex soon turned into Mr Charming, helping me to buy things for my room, setting up my bed.*

All the time he was saying sorry, and telling me he never expected me to forgive him — he just wanted to make sure that I was okay. This phase was unrelenting; he became my saviour, and slowly I forgot that he was the reason I needed saving.

This is why it is so important when someone reaches out for help it is met with understanding and non-judgment. Living with abuse erodes self-confidence; it made me dependant on him, so my inability to cope on my own gave him leverage to keep control over me.

This behaviour makes the abused feel like the abuser intends to make real changes, which adds to the feeling that they have exaggerated prior explosive incidents. In this phase the abuser reconfirms their control over the abused, as the abused feels that they are finally getting the connection they have craved.

The loneliness and isolation that the victim experiences leaves them with nobody to speak to and needing kindness. The abuser then provides this kindness and tenderness, which the abused yearns for, due to the isolation created by the abuser.

This leaves the victim seeing the abuser as their saviour. This perceived closeness further isolates the abused, as they bask in their own private 'loving' bubble. The abused now feels as if their abuser is the safest person in their world, and will get irritated with anyone in their life who tries to burst their bubble and point out that their relationship isn't perfect.

The abused becomes completely enmeshed with their abuser in this phase, and it is quite common that the abused now feels completely in control of both the abuser and the relationship.

The abused will make demands of the abuser, such as insisting on therapy, but as this phase progresses the relationship appears so healthy these demands diminish. It is as if the abuser is 'loving' them into submission.

The abused now feels guilty for telling anyone about the abuse and wants to protect the abuser from the bad opinions of others; they feel as if everything would have been ok if they had just kept their mouth shut. The abused now feels protective of this loving person, and they forget that they are the one who was on the receiving end of the explosive episode. This phase can last days, weeks, months or in some cases years.

Tension Build-up phase

The build-up phase is an unsettling phase for the abused, because they don't want to believe that the relationship they had whilst in the perceived closeness of the entrapment/re-entrapment phase was not real.

The build-up phase will start with little, seemingly inconsequential incidents, like the abuser coming home late without calling, and accusations that the abused partner is being controlling.

This is very confusing, because during the entrapment/re-entrapment phase the abuser would have called, but now they are perhaps a little bit late without calling. It is not a big difference, but there is a shift in energy. The abused feels that they are being paranoid and getting needlessly emotional over such a small thing.

The abuser will act hurt that they are not trusted or because they have been accused of not caring. The abused partner is still in nurturing mode and does not want to upset the abuser, so they will ignore these behaviours.

This lack of respect will increase, but the abused does not want to admit to themselves that the love and care shown to them by their partner was a lie, so they will do what it takes to keep the abuser happy, in order to stop them from facing the reality of this lie. If the abuser comes home late again, it will be overlooked. They will also meet the high demands of the abuser, whether those demands be keeping the home excessively tidy, always looking good, keeping children quiet or overlooking abusive, disrespectful behaviours.

The abused person feels out of control. They feel responsible for the abuser's bad mood, and they worry that they are failing to do what it takes to make the abuser happy. The abuser will start saying mean and cruel things, which will often be disguised as helpful comments. These comments have a cruel precision about them because the abuser knows exactly how to hurt their partner. The abuser has built such a high level of trust that abused has shared all of their vulnerabilities.

This behaviour is so confusing because, on the surface, nothing seems to have changed. Yet the tension in the home is almost suffocating. The abused partner will desperately try to work out what they are doing wrong. Everything they try will be met with derision and criticism, but they cannot face the fact that they are indeed in an abusive relationship. The more the tension builds, the harder they try to get back the 'loving connection'.

The abused partner's every thought is consumed with how to reconnect with their partner. They will berate themselves for being too fat, annoying, unattractive, lazy, useless or any other number of things that they are being accused of being by their abusive partner.

The abused partner is unaware that this is a pattern of behaviour and they are in an abusive relationship. They will drive themselves crazy looking for the way to recreate the perceived connection. What they do not realise is that there is nothing they can do. The abuser is playing with their victim, much like my cat plays with a bug. The abuser lets their partner believe that there is a solution, and that the abused is in charge of the relationship, when in reality it is the abuser that is calling the shots.

Whatever the abused partner tries is met with disapproval, and the abuser will simply move the goalposts. What was right yesterday will be wrong today. This constant shifting of the goalposts ensures that the abused has no time to look at the big picture of how they are being treated, because they are too focused on the small picture of what to do to make their partner 'love' and 'respect' them again. This love and respect was never real, but was just portrayed and perceived as such in the abusive pattern of the entrapment/re-entrapment phase.

The abused partner feels completely alone and isolated because they have shut everyone out of their lives during the entrapment/re-entrapment phase. They now feel too ashamed to tell those close to them what is happening or how they feel for fear of being judged. Often they are unsure of what is happening to them, because domestic abuse is disorientating.

At this stage, many abused people will boast about just how wonderful their relationship is to cover their sense of shame. This further isolates them and leaves their abuser as the only judge of what is 'normal' in the relationship.

The isolation, confusion and desperate loneliness mean they will do anything to make their abuser happy and get back even a glimmer of the love and connection they so desperately crave. Sadly, victims are often unaware or resistant to reaching out to the support and care that is available outside of the relationship. Knowing about these resources can make a life-changing difference, which is why it is important to talk openly about the support your workplace offers.

The more the tension builds, the more desperate the abused becomes. They will start to feel fear and realise they are far from the dominant one in the relationship. They can feel the tension building, and they will desperately try to work out what they can do to prevent it getting worse.

If there are children involved, there will be deep guilt that they have once again allowed this to happen, even though the abused never 'allows' domestic violence to happen; it is not a choice. Those who are being abused will often feel responsible for the abuse. They will try to protect the children and will take on the insults to shield the children.

The tension will continue to build, and the abused partner will start to become fearful even when the abuser is not home. They feel stupid for ever thinking that things would change, and they start to prepare themselves for things to escalate.

There is a deep sense in the abused that they deserve what they get. After all, they have been so demanding — or at least, this is the story they are told by their abuser. If they had only relaxed and enjoyed the relationship, maybe they wouldn't be in this position.

They were not too demanding. They had every right to be in charge of their lives and to expect their abuser to seek help for their behaviour. They are really angry at themselves due to the false belief that they are responsible for this happening.

Stand-over/Intimidation phase

This stage marks the end of the tension build-up phase. All pretence that the abuser feels any compassion or love for their partner is gone. The abuser is now openly aggressive and demanding. As the name would suggest, this is a phase where the abuser literally stands over their partner. This creates great fear for the abused. During the stand-over phase, the abuser will be critical, and the insults will increase both in frequency and nastiness. The abused is starting to forget there ever was a time that they felt connected to their partner.

It is common for the abuser to call their partner constantly with petty demands and insults. They will have impossibly high standards and change their requests frequently. The abused is reeling in this new reality, as their lives spin out of their control. They are heartbroken that the illusion of a loving relationship was not real. They are still trying to put things right and are desperately trying to find a solution to fix the deteriorating relationship. They will grasp for solutions with an increasing sense of panic.

They are completely aware of where this is leading, and they are terrified. The tension is unbearable. They are now completely consumed by the demands of their partner. Functioning in the 'normal' world becomes increasingly difficult, as their mind begins to fracture due to the pressure and fear.

> *I actually functioned well at work, as it helped me keep a sense of control over my life. Work was my safe, happy place. It became harder to maintain any sense of reality once I had left work and was a stay at home Mum. As then my partner became my only locus of what was 'normal'.*

The sense of shame will make them feel a level of self-disgust that is hard for anyone who has not been in an abusive relationship to understand. They think back to the people who have tried to make them see their relationship for what it is and how they dismissed them and shut them out.

They long to reach out and ask for help now, but their shame and belief that they are getting what they deserve mean that in most cases they will not disclose to anyone. They are now frightened, isolated and completely at the mercy of the abuser.

The longer this stage goes on, the more helpless the abused gets, as complete control of their life is taken over. They will be interrogated about the smallest of things, including something as petty as why they spent so long going to the bathroom. No part of their life is spared from this stand-over scrutiny. They will begin to analyse everything they do, from what they cook for dinner to how they cook it, desperately seeking some respite from the oppression of the stand-over phase.

> *The reality is that there is no way to decrease the tension — with the cooking example, there is nothing they can do to alleviate it. If I cooked from scratch, I was accused of being obsessed with food and not wanting to spend time with my partner. If I cooked something simple, I was accused of not caring enough about my partner to cook a proper dinner. If I ordered takeout, I was accused of wasting money. I was in a lose-lose situation and I was completely unaware of it.*

As this phase reaches its climax, the abused becomes increasingly nervous and anxious, to the point that they find it difficult to think straight and see the abuse for what it is. They are still working under the delusion that they have some sort of control over their lives, and that if they could just try harder and not irritate their partner, everything would be fine.

They are so conditioned to the abuse, whilst they know it is wrong, they believe that it is not the fault of the abuser. They focus on their own shortcomings and feel they cannot really blame the abuser for being so angry and frustrated with them.

Without external validation that they deserve love and respect, the abused continues under the false perception that the abuse is their fault.

> *The tension builds until it cannot be contained. For me, the next phase was in some ways a relief, because living under such extreme tension and scrutiny is emotionally, physically and mentally exhausting. Feeling broken and helpless, I now had to find the internal strength to endure the explosive stage.*

Explosion

> *The explosion is when all the tension build-up and intimidation come to a head. As the name indicates, this is truly an explosive time. The explosions I endured left me reeling, separated from reality. Although there had been a build-up, there was still a feeling of shock.*

It is important to note that the explosion is not always physical assault. It could be going missing for days, refusing to pay bills, destroying personal belongings (usually something with sentimental value) or humiliating the abused partner in public. There are many ways beyond physical violence that the cycle of abuse reaches its climax, including rape.

> *Once again, I questioned why this was happening. Self-doubt and self-loathing set in. There was a deep sense of shame that I had let this happen to me. Although the truth was I did not let this happen to me. But I was unaware of the grooming and crazy-making Ito which I had been subjected.*
>
> *This is the point when I realised I had no control over what happened to me in my own home. Although this was the time I most wanted to reach out, it was also a time of such deep shame that I turned inwards.*
>
> *I shut out the very people who could have helped me. I would cancel catch-ups with friends and co-workers. I would pretend to have a wonderful life and seem like the luckiest, most together person. The explosion phase rocked me to the core, and I was analysing what I could have done to avoid it. Without knowing and understanding the patterns of violence, I did not realise that there was nothing I could do.*

Remorse phase, or the 'pretending to be sorry' phase

This phase is difficult to understand for people who do not understand the dynamics of abuse, but it is also hard for the abused person to understand. There are several elements of the remorse stage.

It is important to understand that the remorse is not real, and it is simply part of the pattern of abusive behaviours.

Justification

The abuser will justify their actions by blaming the abused for causing the situation. They will continue to put down and emotionally and verbally assault the abused as a way to justify their actions, although this is done in a remorseful, 'loving' way. This blame, along with the new, 'loving' attitude, adds to the abused partner's confusion.

It is psychologically damaging when someone has done something that is beyond justification, yet they give you a convincing argument for why it was not only necessary, but completely justified.

This kind of justification works because grooming has already taken place, and the abused is accustomed to taking the blame for the abuser's actions.

Minimisation

The abuser will create an environment in which the abused feels like they are overreacting. They will accuse the abused of exaggerating in order to make the abuser feel bad.

The longer the abused person has been in the abusive relationship, the more confusing this tactic becomes. The abused partner knows on an intellectual level that the behaviour and actions of the abuser are wrong. But they have been brainwashed into believing that they do not deserve the same basic rights of safety and care afforded to other people.

They will begin believing they are indeed exaggerating and will begin to feel guilty for their own perceived weakness.

The abuser will often at this time accuse the abused of being attention-seeking and cruel for trying to make them feel bad for a minor incident. Minimising can exacerbate the feeling of isolation and confusion felt by the abused.

Minimisation can have an even more powerful effect when there is no physical abuse, because it is easier for the abuser to blur the lines, leaving the abused more confused and broken as they try to understand what happened to them.

Guilt

Although on the surface this guilt appears real, it is also loaded with blame. The abuser will often explain how the abused caused the explosion. The abuser's guilt becomes the abused partner's burden to deal with.

The best way to explain this is to give a typical conversation

Abuser: I feel so bad. I know it was wrong. I just wish you wouldn't keep pushing me when you know how much stress I'm under.

Abused: Are you really trying to make this my fault?

Abuser: See, I try to apologise, and you just keep trying to make me feel bad. It's like you enjoy seeing me suffer.

Abused: I'm not trying to make you feel bad, I'm just trying to understand why you act like that.

Abuser: See, that's what I've been trying to say. You have absolutely no idea how I feel or what I'm going through. You push me until I snap and then pretend to care. I just wish you loved me the way I love you. Sometimes I can't cope with how you shut me out.

Abused: I do love you, and I never meant to shut you out. You're my life. I hate the thought of you feeling alone. But I don't understand what makes you do the things you do.

Abuser: See, all you care about is one mistake. Maybe if you cared about me instead of this one thing you seem set on making a drama about, I wouldn't feel so used.

Abused: I don't use you. I love you. I have always loved you. I will always love you. Please don't hate yourself. We just need to work harder to be good to each other.

Abuser: Okay, maybe I can try speaking up for myself, and you could try to not be so controlling. Remember that it isn't easy being the one who loves more. Loving you as much as I do overwhelms me sometimes. I am glad that we are talking more openly and you understand how you make me feel.

Abused: Let's move on, and I will try not to be so controlling. We are lucky that we share such a deep love, and I am going to work harder to show you just how much you mean to me.

You can see from that conversation how the abuser has shifted the blame, and the abused person feels responsible for what has just happened to them.

These dynamics can be even more confusing when there isn't physical abuse, as there is no tangible line in the sand between right and wrong. Grooming can normalise this behaviour to the point that the abused person starts to believe that they have imagined it and are overly sensitive.

If the abuse is physical, the abused person knows that a line has been crossed and that it is never acceptable to hit someone. But even then, if violence has become the norm, the abuser will find it easy to play it down and shift the blame for the physical abuse away from themselves and onto the abused.

Pursuit phase

Pursuit and promises

This is the time where the abuser will pursue the abused to make sure they have no time to think or process what is happening to them. They will use their intimate knowledge of the abused to make them feel that the abuser is the best solution for their predicament. In this phase, the abuser will woo the abused, making them feel like the centre of the universe.

Being a victim of abuse means the abused longs for this kind of love and connection. The abused person feels like they are being heard, and they really want to believe that their relationship can be saved.

They are usually too ashamed to tell anyone outside the relationship, so the abuser's actions and words are their only reality. This is a time of making the abused person feel special and admired for the depth of their commitment and their strength in keeping the relationship together.

On the surface, it appears that the abused person is the dominant person in the relationship. But in reality, the pursuit is only there to stop the abused person from gaining perspective, and the promises are empty. The abuser has no intention of changing.

The abuser is simply paying lip-service, because if they had any intention of really making changes, they would seek help to understand their behaviour and do the work necessary to change.

Helplessness

The abuser will use their alleged helplessness to further the illusion that the abused person is, in fact, the dominant one in the relationship. This behaviour appeals to the nurturing nature of the abused.

The behaviour can range from begging that they cannot live without their partner all the way up to threatening suicide. Threatening suicide is a tool abusers use for control in an 'if you won't forgive me, then I might as well be dead' scenario. This behaviour makes sure the abused person has no time to focus on their own thoughts and feelings, because all the attention has been taken up by the abuser's threats of self-harm and helplessness.

The abused person now feels like they have control and it is their job to do what it takes to relieve the abuser's feelings of 'helplessness'. The abused person now has the feeling of control, power and hope. They are losing the feeling of being abused and starting to forget the terror and helplessness they felt during the explosion stage.

The abuser has subtly changed the abused partner's perception of the situation. The abused now feels like a saviour rather than a victim.

But the abused person is still being abused and victimised and these behaviours are part of the abuser's coercive control.

Threats

Threats are used in tandem with helplessness, and they add to the abused person's confusion. One minute, the abuser is completely helpless, and the next they are threatening. It is common for abusers to threaten animals, and suicide also plays a part in this behaviour.

As the abused person is already suffering from learned helplessness, they are an easy target to threaten. Often, they have no financial independence and are scared of being left alone. The abused person often feels like nothing could be worse than the abuser leaving.

These threats confuse the abused person, as they fear being left, and yet they hate what the abuser is doing to them. The abuser flicks through these behaviours so quickly that it is hard for the abused to really get a grasp on what is happening. They go from feeling really strong and in control to being completely frightened.

The tactics used in the pursuit phase are designed to confuse and make the abused feel to blame for what has happened. The abuser is once again gaining control, and the incident is all but forgotten.

One of the threats my partner commonly used was to threaten to tell people how I treated him, what a 'lunatic' I was and how out of control I was at home. This would have blown my cover of appearing to have a perfect life.

I was unsure of what was really happening to me and how much of it I had 'asked for' or deserved. The thought of people finding out, especially my co-workers, was terrifying. I was worried they would think I was weak and/or stupid to let this happen.

The illusion of a good life was all I had left. The thought of losing that was almost too much to bare. I know now there is no way I asked for or deserved to be abused.

It is clear that managers and co-workers must understand the patterns of behaviour in abusive relationships. An employee living with abuse will present differently and have a different understanding of what is happening to them, depending on what treatment and behaviours they are being subjected to at home. They may disclose the abuse during the stand-over or explosion phase, only to clam up and deny anything is wrong when they move into the entrapment/re-entrapment phase. In fact, during that time, they are likely to claim the opposite, and say their relationship is a good one.

If line managers and co-workers understand what is going on for the abused person, they can offer more support and empathy. It will help employees' wellbeing and productivity, as they will be less frustrated and confused by what is happening to their co-worker. If they work in an environment where there is a domestic violence policy and training in place, they will know what help is available, both internally and externally.

When a co-worker suspects or even knows that one of the people they work with is in an abusive relationship, it is a lot of responsibility to carry, and it can even be damaging to the co-worker's own mental health.

Knowledge is power, and education in understanding the patterns of abusive behaviours means employees will have insight into why the abused person is behaving in a certain way, and why that behaviour can so quickly change.

PART TWO

Why is Domestic
Violence a
Workplace Issue?

CHAPTER FOUR

Workplaces: Provide Safe Spaces

The workplace is in a unique and privileged position when it comes to supporting and bringing about positive change around domestic violence. Even though many people assume that domestic violence is not a corporate issue, I can tell you from professional and personal experience this just isn't the case. Outcomes for those subjected to abuse are improved by community support and financial stability. These are two forms of help that employers can provide.

Policies and procedures are important, but on their own they will not bring about the change in culture needed for the companies to support both their employees and customers. Creating an environment that encourages disclosure and enables those going through domestic violence to feel safe and respected is the next step. This can only be achieved through education and understanding. Building empathy instead of sympathy is a productive way forward.

For many people living with an abusive partner, the office is a safe haven. Their workplace gives them eight hours, give or take, of respite, during which their abuser (usually) feels sure of their whereabouts. Therefore, the workplace gives these employees the freedom of physical distance and also emotional and mental space. Immersing themselves in their job gives victims a sense of pride and the familiar. It is part of who they are.

When an employer has created an environment of acceptance and openness, these people will feel more inclined to ask for help. Work really can be the safe space and haven victims need.

There has been a great deal of work done to create a safe space for people to talk openly about mental health in the workplace. In the last decade we have created a different corporate landscape around this issue. This has been good for both employers and employees.

Lack of employment and financial security have a negative effect on an abused person's wellbeing. This financial stress can lead to limited access to long-term medical and psychological care.

By providing robust domestic violence workplace policies and training, companies can help prevent some of the uncertainty around employment and financial security. This support will alleviate some of the stress and anxiety associated with domestic violence.

When in an abusive relationship, a career gives a person grounding and helps them to maintain a positive sense of purpose. Employees who receive support from the companies they work for can keep their focus on their jobs, which helps them financially and emotionally, and enables continuity of employment.

Recovering from an abusive relationship is a rocky road. Employer engagement in training and policies can smooth that path by helping the employee maintain career security. This puts responsibility not just on the company as a whole, but also on those on the front line offering support, to know how to support co-workers dealing with domestic violence.

Imagine if the office was a place where a victim felt safe disclosing their situation. Imagine if, when a victim disclosed such information, they were immediately offered an appropriate response as well as information on the support available to them, both internally and externally.

With the right support, a victim of domestic violence could be empowered to escape their situation. They could even plan their entire exit strategy without changing their regular routine or raising suspicion.

Workplace support could also alleviate the fear of poverty—a fear that often leads a victim to stay with their abuser.

This fear has solid foundations. I left my job before I left my husband, and was unemployed when we ran away and went to the domestic violence shelter. I was healed physically and psychologically years before I was back from the financial abyss.

Remember that domestic violence does not respect—or confine itself to:

- Age
- Socio-economic status
- Race
- Culture
- Religious affiliation
- Gender
- Postcodes
- Sexual Orientation

The people in your organisation dealing with domestic violence are not necessarily recognisable by their position, income or status.

My co-workers presumed I had everything as together at home as I did at the office. This couldn't have been further from the truth.

At home, I was deeply tangled up in brutal domestic violence. My husband abused me verbally, physically and emotionally for more than ten years. I was destroyed.

It is not the picture most people inadvertently paint when they think 'domestic violence victim'. People often imagine a meek woman, an empty-headed woman, a deprived woman.

When I disclosed, my boss believed me immediately and categorically. Unfortunately, because this was many years ago, there were no policies in place and certainly no training available. In fact, I suspect that if my boss had sought advice from her superiors, I would have found myself without a job. But she saved my life. She saved my children's lives. She believed me, and that made me feel I would be heard and believed when I was ready to disclose again.

Financial security and a sense of community

The workplace has the potential not only to change lives but to save them. Two crucial components for someone living in or escaping from an abusive relationship are community support and financial stability. Workplaces can offer both of these.

The people we work with become our extended community, a constant in our lives. This is so valuable when living with domestic violence. Abusers often isolate their partners from family and friends.

There are many ways that abusers do this, including:
- Outright refusal to let the abused see family and friends
- Undermining these relationships, covertly or overtly
- Limiting freedom of movement
- Being rude and making visitors feel unwelcome
- Behaving jealously and attempting to control the abused
- Demanding the abused is loyal to them only
- Refusing to allow the abused to attend sporting, social or religious events

This slow distancing of family, friends and other support networks is confusing and bewildering. Often, the family and friends are blamed for being controlling and trying to break up the relationship.

When you are in the midst of an abusive relationship, it is hard to work out who is on your side. It gets to the stage when you can't trust your own mind.

This is why the workplace is so important. Often, co-workers are the only constant. Work becomes a safe place. When someone is ready to reach out for help, the workplace is often the only support network left.

A workplace that offers support and has developed a

culture of empathy provides an environment where disclosure is safe.

This safety to disclose means employees that are impacted can reach out for help. They are confident that they will be able to maintain employment which may otherwise have been in jeopardy. The financial security that comes along with career security is often the difference between someone leaving an abusive relationship or staying trapped.

As more workplaces implement policies and training to address domestic violence, more people in abusive relationships will be able to make decisions from a position of empowerment rather than desperation. The importance of this cannot be underestimated.

Domestic Violence and Emotional Health

Domestic violence and mental health issues go hand in hand. It is hard to have been subjected to abuse by someone you love without it causing stress. One of the types of abuse is called psychological abuse.

It is important for employers to recognise that these effects are a reality for those subjected to domestic violence. Without support from employers, those affected can easily slip through the net and lose their jobs.

This is not good for the employer or the employee. Lack of employment and financial security have a negative effect on an abused person's wellbeing. This financial stress can lead to limited access to long-term medical and psychological care.

Career Security Means Financial Security

Employers who engage in domestic violence workplace policies and training can help prevent the uncertainty around employment and financial security, which will alleviate some of the stress and anxiety associated with domestic violence.

Financial security also ensures that the abused person has the means to afford the medical support needed to deal with the psychological impacts of abuse.

Although **nobody**—and I mean **nobody**—is responsible for any abuse but the perpetrator, we need to recognise what role we play in ending or enabling domestic abuse.

We are starting to talk about the bystander effect, in which we acknowledge the impact of the bystander in either helping or harming the situation. By getting the bystander to take positive action, we can create positive ripples. It is my view that there are actually one of five roles people can play, and we all get to choose our part:

1. Perpetrator – yes, this behaviour is a choice.
2. Enabler – those who actively cover up, and dismiss and deny the victim's claims of abuse, thereby encouraging abusive behaviours.
3. Bystanders – those who are close to what is going on. Sometimes they may not be sure if abuse is happening, but they also choose not to ask questions.

4. Victim – this is never a choice. Nobody deserves to be abused. No 'but's.
5. Supporter – those who are there for the victim to help them, listen to them, believe them and give support. These people speak out against abuse.

Which role do you fulfil in your workplace?

If you do not think you know anyone in an abusive relationship, it is possible that maybe, just maybe, you are a bystander. Have a look around you.

Think instead about how you can inhabit the role of supporter. The more of us that shift to being supporters, the fewer perpetrators will get away with their unacceptable behaviour.

Speaking out about abuse publicly is hard. I know that from personal experience. But we must speak out if we are to continue to shift the power away from those who use their power and control to abuse others.

Because if:

Victims of domestic violence are in your workplace

Then it stands to reason that:

Perpetrators of domestic violence are in your workplace

If we think about this from the point of view of a company or organisation, there are people from both of these groups in every workplace.

It is easier to think of perpetrators as being some-where over there, where we do not have to deal with them. The truth, however, is they are the people we know in our working lives. To ignore this fact is to ignore an important chance to have a positive impact on domestic violence and at the same time create a more harmonious workplace.

> *When I talk about my ex-partner as a perpetrator of abuse, I am talking about his behaviour at home. He was controlling and psychologically abusive. For a long time in our relationship, he did this covertly.*

Abusers do not leave these behaviours at home and suddenly become nice people with a conscience when they arrive at work. They bring these behaviours with them, creating toxic working environments. Anyone who has worked with or for a bully will know this.

Working for someone who bullies covertly is con-fusing and undermining. The effects ripple through an organisation and pollutes it. We can spend our energy simply getting rid of the perpetrators/bullies from our own backyard, but this does not solve the problem.

Other companies are doing the same, and their perpetrators/bullies are job hunting at your company. We need to acknowledge and accept that there is a problem, and that the problem is nearer than we want to believe. It is hard to think of abusers as our employees and co-workers, but this does not change the fact they are.

The issue many companies are having is, despite having domestic violence policies in place, very few people are disclosing. There are various reasons for this, but not feeling safe in their workplace cannot be overlooked.

Creating cultural change

If we are going to make a positive impact and create a cultural change, we must be willing to look at the issue of domestic violence from all angles. We will discover that workplace bullying is indeed closely related to domestic violence. It is not going to be easy, but the rewards will be worth it.

CHAPTER FIVE

Impact on Your Organisation

Corporate social responsibility – What can your business do?

The answer is 'education'. The more that people under-stand the complexities of domestic violence, the more likely it will be that people will recognise the signs and know what is happening to them or to people in their lives.

> *Schools are starting to educate students about abuse and violence in the home, which is brilliant. I know the difference it would have made to me as a child to know*

what I was being subjected to in my home, constituted child abuse. This would have meant that I had the vital information I needed to make better decisions and choices than I did as an adult. I believe I could have started my healing from the child abuse I was subjected to when I reached adulthood, rather than ending up in an abusive relationship myself.

In reality, teaching our children without also educating adults will not bring about a shift in domestic violence in Australia. It is not children's job to deal with this issue alone! Talking about how hopeless the situation is also won't change it. We have talked about the horrors of domestic violence for years, and they are real. I have lived them. But we need to do more than share stories and say 'stop'. We need to implement policies, training and awareness raising initiatives and make positive change a reality.

We need to educate adults the same way we educate children. Adults are in a position to break the soul-destroying patterns of violence so many families are in. Employees need to understand the dynamics of abuse. Educating adults gives us the greatest chance to make a change for the better. Believe me when I tell you that the cycle of generational abuse is really hard to see, understand and break when you are in it.

This is where corporates come in. They can roll out training programs to their employees so that they know and understand the signs of abuse. Domestic violence is complex. Corporate training, along with domestic violence workplace policies, could bridge this information gap, and if enough companies engage, we could have a completely different outlook within the next couple of decades.

Employees, especially those in abusive relationships, do not need corporates to get emotional on this issue. I would go as far as to say it is the last thing they need. In fact, pragmatic, unemotional but empathetic workplaces who implement training and awareness raising activities are what is needed right now. Corporates are in a truly unique place to help.

There are many ways that companies will benefit by educating their employees about domestic violence, including:

- Staff engagement
- Corporate Social Responsibility
- Increased productivity
- Improved bottom line
- Reduced recruitment costs
- Decreased staff turnover and absenteeism
- A good social license

'An organisation, no matter how well-designed, is only as good as the people who live and work in it' — **Dee Hock**

More and more, the line between work and home is merging. The days of the nine-to-five are over. In fact, for many of us, the only time we truly switch off is on a plane, and now even some of them allow Wi-Fi. There's no time when employees are free to say, 'I cannot be contacted', unless of course we live in France. There are international conference calls at all hours of the night and day. Because we live and operate in a modern world, we accept this as a reality of modern business.

Any successful business knows the truth of Dee Hock's words, 'A business is as good as the people it employs'. With business life increasingly flowing into home and home life flowing into business, the wellbeing of a company's staff is tantamount to productivity and a successful company culture.

Most companies have Workplace Harassment and Bullying Policies and Mental Health Training, and some are implementing Mental Health First Aid. They are doing this because they know it makes good business sense to take care of the most important part of their business—the human part.

For me, both as a survivor and a businesswoman, it is heartening to see so many companies embracing the need for a Workplace Domestic Violence Policy. We have spent far too many years believing the myth that what goes on behind closed doors should stay behind closed doors.

The wind of change is blowing through corporates globally, and I believe there is real power in that wind. If the people with the largest level of power and influence can embrace this change, then it is a good thing for all of us.

But—and it is a big but —this change needs to come with more than just a policy document in HR. Change needs to come with training so employees can benefit from it fully. This training needs to:

- Embrace diversity
- Be non-biased
- Be created and implemented with the complexities of both domestic violence and company culture in mind
- Be presented with the boundaries and needs of the workplace in mind

Companies that create new policies and provide training on this issue will mitigate costs, improve company culture and become industry leaders on this important issue. They will be seen as change-makers: organisations that are willing to look after their people in the most effective ways.

This issue is not going away. Talking openly about domestic violence is now commonplace. As with mental health, this is a topic that will continue to be embraced as the victims' sense of shame diminishes through increased conversation and awareness. More and more people will seek help inside and outside their workplace. So when it comes to discussing domestic violence, it is no longer a hidden and secretive subject. It is now being openly talked about. By accepting this truth, businesses can see their approach to domestic abuse as part of their social awareness efforts.

This is not reinventing the wheel. It is simply evolution and good reasoning. It is adding common sense, necessary policies and training that will benefit the business and its people as a whole.

Cost

Domestic abuse is costing corporates money. Understanding domestic violence and its effects on your business will help mitigate those costs whilst supporting your employees.

The cost and effect on business go further than the bottom line, including:

- Reduced productivity
- Staff absenteeism
- Increased staff turnover
- Lower staff morale
- Negative impact on team cohesion
- Training costs of recruitment

Cost reduction

Corporations can no longer afford to ignore the impact that domestic abuse is having on their business. Yet the costs of domestic abuse in the workplace go much further than economic cost; they extend to corporate culture.

Employees are increasingly looking to work with companies that have a nurturing culture. They want to feel proud of the company they work for. Businesses that have embraced mental health and workplace bullying policies, and provided necessary training and education, have created an environment where real change is possible.

There is no denying that domestic abuse hurts productivity, staff retention and ultimately the bottom line. It is time to stop and look at what domestic abuse is doing to the culture of organisations and the effects it is having on the work environment for key players.

Imagine for a moment being a department head. You have a strong suspicion that one of the people who reports directly to you is being subjected to domestic abuse. But there are no policies or support structures in place, and you're not sure if, or with whom, you should discuss this. So you don't do anything. This is a cultural code of silence.

The code of silence in most workplaces around domestic abuse has an impact on the mental health of the person being abused, their managers and their co-workers. The manager in the example above will be unwilling to seek advice, because they do not know how the person they suspect of being abused will be perceived within the company. The co-workers of the person being abused are probably also aware of what is going on and are themselves unwilling to speak up for the same reason.

If a company has clear domestic abuse policies in place and the training to ensure that employees feel supported, it can help victims as well as their co-workers.

When I was working in corporate, my manager wanted to help. She did as much as she could, given the restriction within the code of silence. I know firsthand that if a domestic violence policy and training had been in place, I would not have left corporate, and they would have retained a key employee.

Home life is no longer separate from work life. The two have become so intertwined that one will always affect the other, so corporations have an obligation to step up.

It is time for them to lead the way, accept corporate responsibly and create not only the policies and training, but also a corporate environment that says we are going to deal with abuse in an engaged, ethical way.

Recruitment costs

When I left my corporate job to move to Australia, I was in a domestic violence relationship. Moving me across the world was the ultimate isolation tactic. In addition, the knock-on effect of losing that position took me a decade to overcome financially.

Only now, when I look back and reflect, do I realise the cost to the company I left. They lost a key employee and the years of knowledge that I brought to my position. They had the task of finding a suitable candidate to take my place.

Anyone in business knows that the cost of recruiting is high, with agencies charging up to 30% of the employee's annual salary. Then you need to factor in the cost of interviewing, including the hours spent interviewing unsuitable candidates and meetings with co-workers about their suitability.

Companies can go down the route of finding an employee themselves, but then hours of billable time will be used to select a suitable candidate from the many applications. Whichever way you go, employing new staff is time consuming and expensive.

Even after you have found a person suited to both your company and the position left vacant because of domestic violence, there is still the cost of training to be accounted for and the loss of productivity whilst the new employee gets up to speed and becomes a fully-fledged member of the team. We all know that building relationships with our co-workers takes time, so productivity is lost across the team as the new member integrates.

In 2011, the Australian Public Service Commission released a report in conjunction with its study, 'Ahead of the Game: Blueprint for the Reform of Australian Government Administration'. It looked at the effectiveness of retention strategies as reported by agencies in 2010–11. The top five things that created effective staff retention were:

1. Study assistance
2. Management or leadership training
3. The inclusion of flexible work practices in industrial agreements
4. Wellbeing programs
5. Internal mobility opportunities

All five recommended strategies would be beneficial for employees subjected to domestic violence, and their managers and co-workers would also benefit from the support available if these policies and strategies were implemented.

Domestic violence is not an easy subject to tackle for anyone, including corporates, but it is not going away. Pretending that it only affects other people is not a solution.

Education around domestic violence will improve staff retention by allowing employees to reach out for help, knowing that the policy and procedures are in place to support them. They will feel safe in the knowledge that they will not be putting their careers in jeopardy by breaking the code of silence.

Reduced absenteeism

When I was living with domestic violence, there were times when I was absent from work due to the stress—often at crucial reporting times, which meant missing deadlines. This obviously had a knock-on effect for both my team and the company as a whole.

This was in turn compounded by my own self-worth issues. On top of constantly being told that I was useless and annoying at home, I was feeling bad at work because I kept letting my co-workers down.

Once my manager knew about my situation, things became much easier for me and for my team. The ability to be honest with my boss meant I was able to concentrate on my job, which increased both the efficiency and accuracy of my work.

There are more reasons for an employee in an abusive relationship to be absent from work than stress. Their partner may be refusing to let them leave for work in the hope of sabotaging their career or from overbearing, controlling jealousy.

They could have bruises or other injuries they are trying to hide, or they may be physically unwell from the abuse. Also, they could have domestic-abuse related appointments with doctors, lawyers, the courts or the bank.

There could be opportunities for them to work from home if it is too difficult for them to come to the office, although home is usually the least safe place for them.

Leaving an abusive relationship is emotionally and logistically time-consuming. Moving and separating from a partner are difficult decisions at the best of times, but given the risk and the need to do the research and groundwork in secret, it becomes imperative that victims can do some of this work in office hours. That way, they are less likely to arouse suspicion.

Team cohesion

After I had disclosed to my boss, she would help me out by making concessions to make my life easier and help me stay on task.

For example, she pulled other team members' deadlines forward so that I would have the information I needed to complete my financial analysis earlier than required. She did this because my partner travelled a great deal for business, and once my partner returned from a trip, I had no idea what I would face or if I would be able to effectively complete the task, so the best plan was for me to complete as many tasks as I could while he was away.

This apparent favouritism did not go down well with others in my team because, of course, they didn't know about the abuse I was subjected to at home. It was not their business. But the bad atmosphere certainly made things more difficult for me. It somehow seemed to justify the vile things my partner said about me. It was not good for me, for productivity or team morale.

It is important, to support employees in a way that minimises further stress and helps maintain team morale and working relationships.

Cyber Security

One of the ways an abuser can gain control is to jeopardise their partner's career. This puts companies at risk of a security breech if the abuser uses private information to create problems for their partner at work.

Supporting employees dealing with domestic violence means knowing that there is a security risk, so companies can take measures to protect their data, intellectual property and social media presence.

Companies need to help employees in this situation to keep their virtual presence secure. Employees are privy to a great deal of confidential and sensitive material about the companies they work for, so helping them to deal with technologically facilitated abuse makes sense, both ethically and economically.

Once an organisation knows domestic violence poses a potential risk, decisions can be made on the appropriate action to take to secure data and company image.

This is an example of a cyber security breech which was disclosed to me. It shows the potential risk.

The abusive partner works for a telco in a senior position. His partner left him and went into hiding; she obtained a violence order. The abusive partner used his position at work to gain access to her phone and internet accounts and removed her authority over her own plan.

Once he had control over her phone he redirected calls and messages to his phone. As the account he had hacked was also an internet account he had access to all the IP addresses, emails and phone numbers used. He knew all her movements and would change appointments and answer emails of her behalf.

All this was done secretly and it was a while before anybody knew. This intimidation went on for months, the abusive partner continually engaged in cyber-hacking, and even hacked a company she was doing business with – the whole company. This was a company that held sensitive, confidential information so this security breech had serious consequences for the abused partner, and the company which was hacked.

It is clear from this example the risk comes from two sides:

1. An employee could get hacked and company data, employee names, numbers and addresses would be vulnerable; if the company gets hacked confidential client and supplier information could also be at risk.
2. If the abuser works for your company there is a risk of them using a work computer – as in the example above – to hack other companies or individuals, leaving the company at risk of somebody contaminating their good name, relationships with clients and/or suppliers or potentially facing a law suit.

By creating an environment which encourages disclosure companies are in a position to see a potential threat and act accordingly.

CHAPTER SIX
What Can Your Organisation Do?

For companies that have not yet incorporated such policies and practices, domestic violence must be added to the agenda—the next agenda. The statistics are staggering. This issue **does** affect you, your corporate culture and your company's productivity.

At the very least, a domestic violence policy should address the chain of command, what leave time is available, how to request leave and up-to-date details of relevant support services.

For those companies that already have domestic violence policies in place, this is a positive step in the right direction. However, policies alone are not enough. How do you make employees aware of the policy? How do you train senior staff to be advocates and to listen openly?

A strong, clear policy that staff are familiar with, and that is easily and quickly accessible, is vital. So too is complementary training.

Training should help people understand domestic violence and its impact, and it should give people the tools as well as the confidence to respond effectively and fast.

Trust me, admitting you are in a violent relationship is not a decision made lightly. It is agonised over.

The reaction you get has a huge impact on whether or not you continue forward on that important, potentially life-saving, path. Any delay when you disclose is an opportunity to second-guess yourself and shut down.

Policies, Procedures and Guidelines

One of the first things that needs to be done is to create policies along with procedures/guidelines. This document will be the benchmark of what support an organisation is going to provide, along with the rights and responsibilities of employees.

Given that domestic violence is an out-of-work issue which is now being supported by the workplace, there are going to be differences when putting a policy together. The policy should cover the following guidelines:

Purpose

It is important to know your purpose for creating the policy. What are the company values and how do you want to reflect them in the policy? My purpose and values are summed up in my mission statement.

To improve the financial outcome for women subjected to domestic violence by empowering businesses with the practical knowledge and understanding about the complexities of domestic violence, in order to create an empathetic environment so that they are able to support them both as employees and customers.

This is at the core of everything I do. My business is run with this ethos. It is important in your own organisations to look at those values and have a clearly defined purpose.

The underlying purpose may change, depending on the area of the business. For instance, what is important to the Diversity & Inclusion team may vary from what a more customer-facing team sees as most important.

When I work with organisations, I get all the key stakeholders together as a first step to get an understanding of how the policy and procedures/guidelines will impact their department. Obviously, from business to business, the relevant departments and therefore the key stakeholders will vary.

Once this information is collated, an overall purpose can be created. It is worth noting that for some organisations it may be necessary to create separate policies for employees and customers.

In my experience, setting up the internal policies and supports first provides a good grounding for the support that will be offered to customers.

Definition

Stating a definition of domestic violence in the policy is important. It may seem obvious but there will be many people in your organisation who do not have a complete understanding of the dynamics of domestic violence. According to the Australian Government's Department of Social Services National Plan to reduce violence against women and their children 2010–2022:

Domestic Violence refers to acts of violence that occur between people who have, or have had, an intimate relationship. While there is no single definition, the central element of domestic violence is an ongoing pattern of behaviour aimed at controlling a partner through fear, for example by using a behaviour which is violent or threatening. In most cases, the violent behaviour is part of a range of tactics to exercise power and control over women and their children, and can both be criminal and non-criminal.

When thinking about the relevant definition for your business or organisation, one thing to consider is the terminology that works for your business. As stated above, there are few variants. For instance, Family Abuse may be your preferred terminology if you are in corporate, but this may not be the best term if you are running aged care homes, as the abuse may not be perpetrated by a family member, but rather a paid carer. So it is important the definition and terminology suit the environment for which you are creating the policy documents.

Responsibility

This is a decision that needs to be made as the policy is rolled out. Who in the organisation is responsible for what, and how is this information going to be shared with all employees? You need to identify who the key stakeholders and decision makers are and what their responsibilities are. These areas include:

- **Employee Disclosure**
  When an employee discloses, it is important that they receive an empathetic supportive response, but it is just as important that they receive the correct information about the resources available to them, both internally and externally.

The employee they disclose to may not have all the information pertinent to their situation, and will need to know who or where to go to for this information.

- **Suspicion that an employee is in an abusive relationship**

  If there is suspicion of abuse, it is vital that those who suspect know who to go to in the organisation for support, information and advice. This will increase the opportunity for them to take the right action steps, whilst caring for their own emotional wellbeing.

- **Customer Disclosure**

  For organisations that have customers who may seek support, employees need to know what internal support is available and who can sign it off. This needs to be easily accessible to ensure a timely response.

  Reaching out for help is difficult, and delays can mean victims feel that they are not believed. They may close up and stop seeking help, which can ultimately be dangerous.

- **Suspicion that a customer is in an abusive relationship**

  This is a sensitive area and needs to be handled with care. Front-facing employees require guidelines that are both comprehensive and easily accessible, along with a clear chain of command, so they know who to reach out to when the situation arises.

- **Case Escalation**

Domestic violence is not a one-cap-fits-all situation, and some people will need more support than others. Employees need to clearly understand who to go to if the support required is more than they are trained to offer. Where do they escalate the issue to, and what is the procedure for doing so?

- **Compliance**

The Domestic Violence Workplace Policy will likely overlap with other policies like Occupational Health & Safety (OH&S), Workplace Bullying and Critical Incident policies, to name a few.

It is important that compliance is kept up-to-date and employees are aware of the impact on other polices when they are looking at the Domestic Violence Workplace policy.

- **Cost of Implementation**

Domestic Violence Workplace policies and ongoing training come under many areas of the business, and from the outset it makes sense to decide which department is paying for what when it comes to roll-out.

Progress is often hampered by indecision on whose budget the costs will be taken from. Having plans and ideals is good first step, but who is taking accountability for the cost of implementation?

- **Support**

Another decision that needs to be made is what support the organisation is going to offer employees. There are various things that can be offered. Some of these are:
  - Paid leave to attend appointments related to the abuse, including medical and legal appointments, along with issues relating to children.
  - Relocation – if viable
  - Financial support
  - Employee Assist Program (EAP)

There are other things managers can do to assist

1. Managers can help put a safety plan together, from a caring but detached perspective. Being too emotionally involved can be a negative when assisting with a safety plan.
2. Keeping certified copies of important documents, such as passports, birth certificates, driving licenses, etc.
3. Having an alternative emergency contact on file in case the employee goes missing or is in danger.
4. Redirecting wages for the short-term to a bank account that is unknown to the abusive partner.

Support that can be offered to customers will vary depending on the industry of the organisation.

Confidentiality

Confidentiality is really important. This is a big subject, but for the purposes of this book, it is essential to think about OH&S policies and employee welfare when thinking about confidentiality. Does keeping the issue of abuse quiet endanger other employees or the employee disclosing?

There may be a need to disclose the situation without naming the employee involved. Looking at the overall implications of a blanket confidentiality agreement will mean workplaces can place the safety of all employees in the decision process.

Policies, procedures and supervisor training are necessary to help victims come forward

It is important to understand that there is no 'type' when it comes to who will be in an abusive relationship. Human resource professionals and managers will likely not be able to predict or intuit on their own who is a victim of abuse. This is why it is so important to create a conducive environment so that employees will feel comfortable disclosing their situation.

Paid leave

There is a good deal of conversation going on around the subject of domestic violence leave at the moment. I am in favour of this form of leave, due to my own personal and professional experiences. I believe that paid domestic violence leave must be a part of the solution to domestic violence.

There is so much talk about people using this leave as extra holiday, or as a new way to 'throw a sickie'. Companies are not setting this up to be an extra ten days' leave. If you wanted extra leave, there are much easier ways to get it.

Will there be the few that work the system, to gain extra time off? Of course. But that is where training comes in. Companies are training their staff to understand the complexities of domestic violence and how to support employees affected. Understanding the support the company offers means that the right leave can be offered to the right people.

Domestic violence leave is designed to create space for the employee going through domestic abuse to have the time to deal with immediate issues of safety. This leave creates time to see solicitors, make police statements, attend court and visit the doctor, attend to the needs of children, (new schools for example) and other things.

When I work with my clients, I suggest they offer what I call 'working leave' because (as I have mentioned before) work can often be the safe space for someone being abused. Working leave means they can come to work as normal, thus not alerted their abuser that they are reaching out for help.

They can use this time with a computer and phone that their abuser can't trace to makes calls and plans for leaving. This gives them the time, space and importantly, the safety, to work out the best plan for them.

> *If I had taken a day's leave my partner would have known somehow that I didn't go to work, even without today's technology. This technology and tracking devices make it vital that normal routine is maintained. Leaving is the most dangerous time, and to make plans without raising suspicion is an important part of safety planning.*

This leave is usually signed off by the day or even the half-day. In the companies I have dealt with, it is not seen as an extra two weeks' leave. Instead, it enables an employee to be honest about the support they need and offers them the time to create a safe way forward.

Having a set amount of leave may not be viable for smaller companies, but they can still encourage open communication and be flexible with working times so employees can attend to the things they need to.

Living with an abusive and controlling partner is all-consuming, and finding the time to have a free thought is difficult. The best way an abusive partner has to make sure that power is complete is to control every aspect of their partner's life. Paid leave balances out that power and puts some control back in the hands of the victims.

This leave makes sense:

For Businesses

Losing key employees impacts productivity, and it increases recruiting and training costs. Staff retention is important, and paid leave will mean employees have the support they need to maintain their employment.

For Government

Surely it is easy to see how the government will benefit from this. If an employee is supported and maintains their employment, they also maintain their role as a taxpayer. Instead of the victim losing their job and becoming reliant on the government, they are actively putting money into this country. That is money that can go towards helping those who so desperately need it.

For the Not-for-Profit Sector

This sector is so under-funded and overstretched in the domestic violence area. The more we can keep people to stay in work, and move away from the poverty domestic violence can cause, the more money there is for those who depend on these services.

For Victims

Financial security is so important for rebuilding a life after domestic violence. It is a prevalent factor in why people stay in abusive relationships. Support from an employer whilst dealing with domestic violence, including paid leave, can make the difference. People do not want to rely on charity and government for financial support. Paid domestic violence leave is one of the tools to help ensure that this does not happen.

Perpetrators are the only ones not to gain from this because paid leave will give their partners the time and space to gain the confidence and information needed to break the chains of the abuse. Surely, making sure nobody cons an extra day of work is not more important than offering the necessary support so that someone can break out of violence and potentially save lives.

Safety plan

For those in abusive relationships, it is hard to cognitively deal with all that is happening. This makes planning to leave difficult. By the time the victim is ready to leave, they are broken down physically, mentally and emotionally. Often, they are too exhausted to even contemplate the future. Just getting through the day is challenging enough. If a victim has to leave in a hurry, it is hard to think about what is important. Some even have to leave in a hurry in the middle of the night in their pyjamas.

Setting up a safety plan in advance can make a big difference. It means that before there is a state of urgency, a plan can be thought through.

Here are some things to be considered for a safety plan:

- Where will they go?
- How will they get there?
- Who can they trust?
- Do they have a safe word that only those who are trusted know?
- Can they take the car? If yes, is it safe to hide a spare set of keys somewhere?
- Do they have copies of important documents?
- Do they have a spare phone that is not traceable by their partner?
- Who is recorded as their emergency contact in their personnel file?

There are many other things to consider when putting together a safety plan, but the most important is safety. Is it safe to have bags packed? Or to have copies of documents hidden in the home, etc.?

If you enter the words 'Domestic Violence' and 'Safety Plan' into your search engine, example safety plans will come up.

Domestic Violence and Mental Health

The support being offered to employees under the Domestic Violence Workplace Policy may overlap with other policies, e.g. Health and Wellbeing Policies, as domestic violence and mental health issues often co-exist. Consideration needs to be taken when allocating costs to ensure they are not duplicated.

Where there is domestic violence there are often related mental health issues that the employee is contending with. It is hard to have been subjected to abuse by someone you love without it causing stress.

One of the types of abuse is psychological abuse. We talk about 'crazy-making' because this is the aim of this abuse— to make the abused person doubt their own mind. These gaslighting behaviours of the abuser are purposely confusing.

Abuse—and the confusion it causes—can seriously harm a victim's health and wellbeing, often for a long period of time, which in turn will impact their productivity. Some of these effects are:

- **Stress**
- **Anxiety**
- **Depression**
- **Sleep disturbances**
- **Eating disorders**
- **Homelessness**
- **Poverty**

A supportive workplace will assist in mitigating some of these effects, which is good for those impacted and also makes good business sense.

Supporting employees makes economic sense

It is a win for the government to help victims of abuse, because it enables people to stay in work and continue as taxpayers rather than ending up on welfare. When we think of the costs associated with domestic violence, surely supporting workers to stay in employment is a more cost-effective way to deal with these costs.

When we look at the cost of recruitment and the impact on productivity, it makes sense for both corporate and government to proactively support those dealing with domestic violence.

This issue requires community organisations, healthcare providers, not-for-profit organisations, federal, state and local governments and corporates to do what they can to support those suffering and create the change needed for future generations. This is why we must keep the conversation going, and implement training and awareness-raising measures.

PART THREE

Spotting the Signs
and Communicating

CHAPTER SEVEN
Signs That You Are Being Abused

The following are signs that your husband, partner, wife, boyfriend or girlfriend, your carer or family member, co-worker or boss is abusing you.

In this chapter I have used stories from my life or others I know, or from professionals who have shared (without mentioning names). I do this to give you an insight into how it feels inside an abusive relationship, and that understanding creates true empathy.

They make you feel uncomfortable

This is a difficult feeling to define, because it will look different depending on the people in the relationship. What makes me uncomfortable will not make others uncomfortable. The difference is that when it is someone close they know what will make you uncomfortable yet deny it is happening and it makes it difficult to trust your own feelings.

> *My partner claimed to love me and to be my best friend, but I always felt on edge, like I was unsafe. He would share my secrets and then claim not to know they were private. I could not relax around him. He dismissed this as paranoia and my lack of ability to trust.*

If you or someone you know is uncomfortable with their partner, don't dismiss it. The people who claim to care about us should make us feel safe and loved. If this is not the case, you need to question why. More importantly, you need to question why you cannot discuss it with your partner.

They put you down, make fun of you, humiliate you or make you feel worthless

This behaviour can look and feel like harmless fun at first. But a constant barrage of being put down erodes confidence and a sense of self.

> *My ex would 'joke' that I was either too chatty or not chatty enough. He claimed that I always needed to be the centre of*

attention. He would go on and on, sometimes in the guise of a joke and other times as if he was trying to guide me to be better at making friends.

If I called him out on it, he would tell me I was too sensitive and I couldn't take a joke, which would be evidence I needed help making friends. After a time, I doubted my own worth and started to find it difficult to make friends. This added to my isolation and increased his power over me.

My friends and co-workers would often ask me why I was always so quick to defend him when he was rude or humiliating to me. I would always say, 'He doesn't mean it, I don't mind.'

When somebody is overly accepting or defensive of their partner's insults or put-downs, I will subtly tell them that it is not okay to be treated like that, because I see this as a sign that the relationship may be an abusive one.

They persistently check up on you and need to know where you are all the time

At the beginning of the relationship, this can seem romantic. It feels nice to be wanted. But the need to know your whereabouts quickly moves onto controlling your movements. Someone who needs to constantly know the whereabouts of their partner, and tries to control where they go and who they see, is engaging in controlling and abusive behaviour.

> *When I was first with my abusive partner, he would travel a lot. I thought it was romantic, but he would call me all the time and say that he wanted to spend time with me alone. I couldn't see it then, but this was the start of his isolating me from my friends. I would say no to plans if he and I were having a 'phone date'. At the time, I thought this was very romantic.*

They convince you that nobody will believe you

This is part of the crazy-making; attempting to get the victim to minimise the abuse and push blame onto themselves. This is done to maintain control and to ensure their victim does not reach out for the support they need.

> *After one particularly brutal beating, I phoned my friend in England. She managed to talk me into going to the Sydney airport. I booked into a hotel, and she was willing to pay for my flight home. He persuaded me to tell him where I was, and he came to get*

me. I told her I would be fine and that I was staying.

After that, he convinced me that my friend thought I had made the whole thing up for attention, and that she was really annoyed that I had wasted the money she spent on the hotel. I was so sure he was telling the truth I avoided her for months. This was untrue. In reality she was scared for my welfare. Once again, he was isolating me from my friends.

They limit your access to money

Controlling finances is an effective way to gain control over a partner. This happens even when the controlled partner is in work and is earning. Lack of financial independence limits options. Without money, the abused becomes essentially dependent.

My partner would transfer all of our money onto his American Express card. I had no access to the funds once they had been transferred, which left me without any money. I often had to beg for basics like nappies and food. This was in part so he would have more funds to sustain his partying lifestyle, but was also a way to control where I went and what I did.

It is hard to function if you have no access to money.

They isolate you from friends and family

There are many ways to isolate someone from friends and family, many of which are covert. These include blocking calls, undermining friendships, spreading rumours about friends and family, making people feel unwelcome when you invite them over or being rude when others invite you places.

Eventually, people stop extending invitations, leaving the abused partner with a very limited social circle. This can have a negative impact at work when it occurs for events arranged by co-workers, as the abused can become isolated from the social network within their workplace and therefore the support network that they need.

My friends told me after I left him for the final time that they had always found it weird that, although my partner worked in IT, I never had an email address I could access, and that my phone always seemed to need repairing.

I now know that he chose not to connect my email or give me passwords in order to control my access to the people who were supportive of me. My texts and calls were frequently forwarded to his phone without my knowledge.

Often my friends would get tired of inviting me places only to be ignored, so they stopped inviting me. They thought that I did not want to spend time with them.

They make you feel scared to disagree or say no

This is not necessarily fear of physical repercussions, although there may be an element of that. This fear comes from being subjected to the behaviours mentioned earlier in the book. It means the victim is always second-guessing themselves, and lives in fear of upsetting and/or angering their partner.

It becomes so that the partner's happiness is always paramount to the abused, which leaves them feeling ashamed and disempowered, often without understanding why.

Once someone has control over you, it is no longer an equitable relationship. This changes how you react in the relationship.

I remember we were going away for the weekend to a function for the company I worked for at the time. We went dress shopping, and he wanted me to get a designer dress. Even though I love designer dresses, I didn't love the one he chose for me. It was canary yellow and really short. I felt really uncomfortable in it. I did not want to buy it and certainly did not want to wear it to my work function. I tried to say no, but he became angry saying, 'You are such an ungrateful bitch.' I was too scared to stand up to him, so I ended up wearing it.

My friends still talk about how uncomfortable I looked in that dress.

They threaten that you will lose your children

This is a reality for many in abusive relationships — they do end up losing custody or the abusive partner gets joint care, meaning the victim is now left with a situation where, if they leave, they will not be in a position to protect their children. Fear for the children's safety is one of the reasons it is so difficult to leave an abusive relationship.

I was constantly called 'insane' and 'a lunatic'. Eventually, I believed it. He would then use this to convince me that without him I would have my children taken away, because I was so unstable.

My belief that this would happen was so strong that when I entered the domestic violence shelter I was convinced that my children would be taken away, but I knew

I had to get them away from the abuse, whatever the cost to me.

They pressure, force or trick you into doing things sexually that you don't want to do

This happened to me more times than I care to remember, and I do not feel comfortable writing about it in this book, but I will say the emotional scars it left took a very long time to heal.

They warn you that you will be alone if you leave

As much as living in an abusive relationship is hard, the thought of being alone and managing by yourself, after years of being broken down physically, mentally and emotionally, can seem overwhelming, if not impossible.

Having created a dependence and learned helplessness, he then told me that no one else would ever want me and I would be alone forever.

They threaten to leave if you don't do as they say

I was so convinced that I was too broken to cope on my own that he would threaten to leave me as a way to control me. The thought of being on my own absolutely terrified me. This became a very effective way to control me.

They hurt or threaten to hurt you if you leave

This is a valid concern, as the time of escaping and the six months afterwards are the most dangerous times in an abusive relationship, so it is important to take these threats seriously; a safety plan is a must.

This is where employers can make a real difference, as the more informed and supported someone is, the more likely they are to have a good outcome.

These are other signs, which include:
- **They abuse you in front of children**
- **They hurt or threaten the children**
- **They hurt or threaten to hurt pets**
- **They hurt or threaten to hurt family or friends**
- **They scare and hurt you by being violent**

CHAPTER EIGHT
Signs that a Co-worker is Being Abused

The following are signs to look out for if you suspect a co-worker, friend or family member is being abused. Remember, those being abused are good at concealing the abuse, so the signs may not be immediately obvious. If you have a feeling, trust your instincts and reach out and gently and tactfully start a conversation.

Neglecting, improving or in any way changing the way they look or dress

This may be starting to make less effort with their self-care and clothing, as their partner does not like them to look attractive. Or, it could be they are too tired and worn down to care. However, they could be being forced/coerced into dressing more glamorously. They may be seen as property by their abuser, who wishes to show them off.

> *For me, I became more glamourous. It was important to him that I always looked the part. I often wore more makeup and more revealing clothes than I had in the past. Looking back, I can see he liked me feeling uncomfortable as it made him feel powerful.*

There could be evidence of physical injury or emotional distress, and the abused person may tell lies to cover it up.

> *Often my physical wounds would be in places on my body that were not easy to see. Even when they were visible, I would make excuses, to protect him and also to hide the shame I felt about how I was treated in my home.*
>
> *My eyes would often be red and swollen from crying. I started to pretend I had hay fever, although it is not something I suffered from. I still find myself saying I used to get hay fever when I lived in England, and then I remember that I didn't. I told this lie so often it still almost seems like the truth.*

When talking to someone who has injuries that are inconsistent with their story, be gentle, but let them know that you are ready to listen and assist in getting them help when they are ready. Be very careful not to be pushy. It will only make them retreat from you.

Clothing could change to disguise evidence of physical abuse

If a co-worker occasionally covers up and wears scarves, tights or trousers when this is unusual they may be trying to cover injuries sustained in the violence. Scarves and tights or stockings are an indicator if the weather is hot and the clothes seem out of season.

> *I would often wear a different outfit from the one I intended to wear, even when I had bought it especially for the occasion. This was often to hide a bruise or a mark he had inflicted on me.*

Changes in social behaviour/increased isolation

> *The longer I was with my abusive partner, the less sociable I became. I would actively avoid social situations that I had once enjoyed and embraced. I was never told I could not go out. Rather, I was undermined, and I lost the confidence I needed to be sociable.*

At the same time, he would twist my thoughts around friendships I had. It got to a point where I trusted nobody, including myself.

If you notice a change in someone's social behaviour or see that they are isolating themselves, take the time to chat with them. Start a conversation, tell them you are worried about them. Ask if there is anything they need from you. Invite them to open up to you. Make it clear you are coming from a place of non-judgement. Try not to be intrusive, because this may mean they will shut down. But let them know you are there for them if they want your support or somebody to listen to them.

Living with an abusive partner leaves people feeling ashamed and often reluctant to disclose. The important thing is to create a safe space for them to open up.

They lack the confidence they used to have

This really feeds off the last point. Withdrawing and losing confidence are signs that something is wrong. Remember, it is not necessarily due to family violence. They could be being bullied or harassed in the workplace.

Again, open a channel of communication with them. Let them you know they can speak with you.

Disinterested, preoccupied, distracted or in a hurry

My partner used to travel a great deal. When he was home, I found it difficult to concentrate on anything but his over-whelming demands on me. Things I had always enjoyed, including at times my work, were of little or no interest to me. I just did not have the mental or emotional energy to spare.

I would often be in a hurry, either because I did not want to answer what were—given my situation—intrusive ques-tions. Often, I was in a genuine hurry because I knew he would be annoyed if I was late.

Constantly checking their phone and seeming stressed

I remember being at a friend's hen night, and my partner kept calling. My friends ended up taking my phone off me, giggling and saying he could manage one night without me. I was terrified because I knew how angry he would be if I ignored him.

If someone seems agitated when their partner calls or if they cannot answer, this can be a sign that they are being controlled by their partner.

Avoiding talking about their relationship/home life

Not wanting to discuss their home life or relationship beyond the most superficial level could be a sign of something being wrong, especially if this is new behaviour. However, remember that some people are by nature very private.

Social media and communication habits change

Changes in their social media activity or profile that seem out of character can be a red flag. The same goes for changes in the way they communicate or the openness of their communication.

> *I left my abusive relationship before social media had become what it is today, but I do know that I became less interactive. I would reply to texts, but stopped initiating contact, either by phone or in person.*
>
> *Sometimes, depending what was happening in the patterns of behaviour, I would go back to being really sociable. However, it never lasted, and I would soon withdraw again.*

Old relationships break, and the person avoids things from the past

I started to avoid my own friendship groups and co-workers in favour of his. I remember leaving a job, and at least forty co-workers coming to my leaving dinner. My ex-partner was in the pub where we were all having drinks before going to dinner. He told me that when we left the pub literally emptied.

I see looking back how he undermined me from the moment I started my new job. I didn't make anywhere near the friendships I had made in previous workplaces.

Again, changing or avoiding past activities and friendship can be a red flag.

Having no access to money

Although I was in a well-paid job, I rarely had access to money. My partner would spend most of the money, and I would be left to pay the mortgage, bills, food and other essentials. After I left him, I learned that he was telling everyone I didn't want to go out because I thought I was better than them.

At the same time, he was telling me they all seemed relieved I wasn't there and that it hurt him that my friends didn't like me. No wonder my friendships fell apart.

Reactions and emotions don't seem real or to match the situation

Weirdly (or maybe not weirdly) the example that comes to mind is my wedding day. The day I got married, I was not happy. I was unsure whether or not to go through with the wedding, but I didn't understand why.

My friends and family have said since then that the wedding felt like a funeral and that they could feel the sadness in me. I had moved to Australia six months prior, and I was returning straight after the wedding. They attributed my sadness to that. But I love Australia; it was never my problem.

If somebody's emotional responses don't seem to match the situation, don't presume anything. Instead, open dialogue with them. Even if they are not ready to listen yet, maybe you can sow a seed for them.

Workplace-specific behaviours

Uncharacteristic lateness

Changes in working patterns, be it lateness or staying later, can be signs of abuse. Lateness can be due to lack of sleep due to the abuse. They may need longer than usual to get ready in the morning to cover up injuries.

Their abuser could be restricting access to the family car at the last minute or hiding/stealing travel cards, credit cards and money, making it difficult for the abused person to get to work.

Changes in working patterns

They may start working longer hours because they are avoiding home and therefore their abuser. Often work is a safe haven, and those in an abusive relationship may be reluctant to go home. If this is consistent, it is worth a conversation about their apparent resistance to going home.

It could also be that they are struggling with their workload due to the mental and emotional demands the abuse is placing on them. It may only be in the perception that they are not doing a good job, but because of the constant put-downs at home they have lost confidence in their abilities.

The abused may be frightened of losing their job if their work is not up to usual standard, and they may work longer hours to compensate. Again, open up dialogue with them, because even if it is not due to abuse, this is certainly an indication that they are under stress.

Frequent absences from work

A person suffering from abuse may take more leave than normal due to the abuse, or they may opt to work from home more in order for injuries to heal.

> *Psychological abuse makes it difficult to think. There were days I stayed at home because I was scared I would make decisions that would be counter-productive for me, my team and my company.*

Decreased productivity

> *People I worked with used to tease that I would get twice as much work done when my partner was travelling than when he was home. The joke was that I partied too hard when he was home. There was an element of truth to that, as partying was something that I was expected to do. However, the partying alone would not have been a problem. It was coping with the abuse I was subjected to when he was home that meant I struggled to concentrate, as it had a negative effect on my cognitive abilities.*

Decreased productivity can be a sign of abuse. It is a particularly stressful one, because often work is the one place a victim still feels like themselves.

High levels of anxiety around their partner

I was constantly walking on eggshells when I was with my partner. But it didn't always look like fear. I would often say things that I did not mean, or laugh at things I didn't find funny because I was scared to upset him. This fear, along with the change in my personality around him, was a sure sign.

Receipt of unexpected gifts

Someone receiving gifts, especially an unusual number of gifts for what appears to be no reason, can be a sign. Also, if their reaction to those gifts is inconsistent with the gesture, it is another sign of abuse.

This is part of the re-entrapment phase. Whilst on the surface it seems 'romantic', it is overwhelming and intimidating. Over-the-top gift-giving is controlling, as it does not allow the abused the space they require to think, which is one of the reasons why the abuser does it. The gifts also serve as a barrier between the abusive behaviour and the present behaviour of the abuser. The abuser will often become enraged if their 'apology' gifts are not 'sufficiently appreciated' by the abused partner.

Partner appearing at the office

If a partner frequently and unexpectedly turns up at the office, this can be a sign of abuse, especially if it makes the victimised partner feel noticeably uncomfortable.

Repeated references to problems in the relationship

If someone repeatedly talks about problems in their relationship, only to minimise it later, it is a sign something is wrong.

I would often tell people I was unhappy in my relationship, although not about the abuse directly. To be honest, I did not really recognise it as abuse at the time. I would often then change my story and blame myself for all the difficulties in the relationship, due to both embarrassment and guilt at having spoken out.

Making excuses for the partner

This was a big one for me. I would be the butt of his jokes, which were often crude and humiliating. I would always laugh it off as if I found it funny. If someone called him out on his behaviour, I would be the first one to make excuses.

Whatever he did, I would make excuses. I would excuse the inexcusable.

If someone is defending behaviour that is unacceptable, maybe they don't even realise how bad it is. Privately say to them, 'You do know this is not okay, don't you?'

Reluctance to leave the children alone with their partner

This may come up as a work issue if an employee is resisting overtime or changing hours even though their children are with the other parent. Try not to immediately judge them as unwilling to cooperate. They may be fearful to leave their children with their partner.

CHAPTER NINE

Communicating with a Colleague in an Abusive Relationship

Discussing domestic violence in the workplace is not easy, but it is important that employees and customers feel heard and believed. The reaction an abused person gets the first time they disclose their situation can be the difference between safety and staying in a dangerous situation. This can make it intimidating to think about having those conversations.

These conversations are new to the workplace, and it is important to recognise the role played when you are the one chosen for disclosure. How you react is as important as what you say.

Empathy is so important, as is understanding domestic violence and the ways that it erodes a person's sense of self. Recognising this helps you to understand the complexities of the issue.

Chances are that the person disclosing doesn't really understand what is happening to them, having had their abuser minimise and justify the abuse for the duration of the relationship. So, if the first person they confide in doesn't seem to believe them, it can be taken as a sign to close up again and 'stop making a fuss'.

They may not speak up again for a long time, which gives the abuser time to regain control. Once this control has been re-established, it could be months, if not years, before the victim has the confidence and headspace to reach out again. The memory of past disclosures not going well can erode the much-needed confidence.

When an employee or customer is disclosing abuse, remember the following points:

- Listen without judgment
- Ask what they need from you
- Ask about their immediate safety
- Determine if they have a safety plan
- Let them know you believe and support them
- Know your limitations and boundaries

There is so much to think about when dealing with someone going through domestic violence. Acknowledge that it is a difficult subject to discuss, and if you have no previous experience, it is okay to say so. This way, instead of thinking you are judging and disbelieving them, they will understand how difficult the situation is, which in itself can be validating.

Remember that you are not their therapist. This is not your role. If your company has an EAP (Employee Assist Program), you can give your co-worker the details. It is important to have at hand information about your company's policies and procedures and information about appropriate external resources and helplines. So before you are in a position of having the conversation, make sure you are equipped with the information you need and can give your co-worker your full attention.

Importance of training

> *I have often fantasised about there being domestic violence policies when I was working in corporate at the same time as being in an abusive relationship. Would that support have meant a different outcome for me? Could I have kept my career? Would I have had the support I needed to leave my abusive partner earlier?*
>
> *I had a boss who knew and was supportive. Back then, her going to HR was not really an option, as they probably would*

not have been helpful. Abuse in the home was not something that was discussed; it was a secret to be kept locked behind closed doors.

In the past few years, this has changed globally. Violence in the home is now something we are more open to discussing. A growing number of businesses worldwide now have domestic violence policies, in which they offer support to their employees. Given my past and how much the support of my boss meant to me, it is hard to put into words just how grateful I feel that this is now the environment in which those subjected to domestic violence are working.

Good communication is key

Being in an abusive relationship is confusing, primarily because of the effects of emotional and psychological abuse. When I left my abusive partner, I was unsure if what I had been through even constituted abuse. Looking back now, this seems incredible, but because my partner regularly minimised my feelings, I doubted my own perceptions.

Imagine someone in that state of mind going to a manager who doesn't feel comfortable talking about domestic abuse and has no clue what to say. The employee seeking advice could see it as a sign they are exaggerating, or worse still, they are not believed.

This could create a situation where the victim feels they were wrong to seek support, it would have been better to stay quiet, and the policies are for those who are 'really' going through abuse. This could prevent them from seeking further support, leaving them trapped and isolated in an abusive relationship.

My boss was so supportive. She helped me find somewhere to live and went above and beyond for me, even though she did not have any formal training and did not realise that it takes on average between seven and thirteen attempts to leave an abusive partner. There was a statistically high chance of my returning to my abusive partner, which I did.

This led to a communication breakdown. I felt like I had let her down because years of abuse had led to a belief that it was my job to please. My boss felt like she had forced me to leave my partner. This led to awkward encounters in hallway, meetings, and tea rooms.

In meetings, we would consciously try not to sit anywhere that would involve eye contact. Ultimately, I left my job because I was embarrassed and ashamed. Neither of us had the skills to communicate about the abuse I was living with.

Managers should not be encouraged to have conversations that they are not trained to handle. It is essential that companies teach managers to understand the complexities of domestic violence, including the signs they should look for and how to effectively communicate with victims of abuse. Policies are one side of the coin; training is the other.

See the person, not the problem

Domestic violence has no boundaries and can touch anybody, regardless of their education, religion, socio-economic status or community. There is often a presumption privilege will somehow provide immunity from abusive relationships. People with a long, successful corporate career can suffer in an abusive relationship. There is no immunity.

Fear of disclosure

One of the challenges for an abused person is the fear of not being believed. On the surface, a co-worker may appear to have it all: money, security and career. But abuse is abuse, and behind closed doors their life is anything but safe and secure. It is challenging to help victims of abuse feel safe and supported enough to speak up, but I am proud to say that companies are now tackling this challenge.

When talking to someone who has disclosed, or whom you suspect of being in an abusive relationship, try to put yourself in their position. Imagine disclosing something really personal and private to a work co-worker, especially something of which you are not proud.

As obvious as it may seem on the outside of an abusive relationship that it is never the victim's fault, those in an abusive relationship have a tendency to blame themselves. I was no different. In fact, it took years for me to understand what had happened to me and realise that it was not my fault.

Joint finances make leaving difficult

Domestic abuse occurs even in wealthier socio-economic communities. For people in this situation, financial abuse can have severe consequences. If you are carrying a large debt or mortgage in joint names, how do you leave without facing financial ruin? Trust me when I say, 'It is a long journey back from financial ruin.'

So even though the person you are talking to may be high up in your organisation and on good money, finances could still play a role in the reason they stay. It is important not to presume when discussing domestic violence with someone.

For financial institutions it is important to recognise customers and clients who may need help with the issues surrounding joint finances when leaving an abusive relationship.

Disclosure in the workplace was hard and felt humiliating.

When I disclosed in my workplace, I was unsure if what I had been through was even abuse. I was scared to speak out, but I was equally scared to keep quiet. My life was spiralling out of control. I was trapped in an abusive relationship.

I am grateful for my boss's support and will be grateful for the rest of my life. Her validation and care changed something inside me. It may have taken years for me to finally leave, but I do not underestimate the importance of the reaction to my first disclosure.

I felt heard and valued, and I understood that I was more than my problems. It was difficult to disclose at work, as it was the one area in my life where I felt that I was achieving. I never meant to disclose. It came out unintentionally. I feared my career was over and that I would be seen as weak and pathetic. How would I ever be respected again?

My boss believed me and did everything she could to help me, even helping me to buy a bed. But neither of us had any idea about the complexities of abuse. So after helping me to leave, neither of us could understand why I would quickly return. The dynamics created in the abusive relationship with my partner were not something I nor my boss understood.

Remember boundaries are important. Crossing boundaries can compound the situation and put you in a difficult position. It is not your job to save them; there are support services for that. Even in the absence of internal workplace supports, there are external supports available (see Appendix I Seeking Help and Key Statistics).

We are at the beginning when it comes to dealing with domestic violence, but I believe we can make a huge positive impact on the frightening statistics. Companies are at the forefront of that.

Listening

The most important thing in listening is to have an open mind and empathy. Empathy will help the person you are talking with feel heard and encourage further communication. Listen with the aim of understand what they are dealing with and what support they need from you. There are some basic do's and don'ts:

The Do's

- Thank them for trusting you
- Let them know that you believe them
- Ask them how you can help them
- Ask them why they chose you. Be sure you are the one they want to disclose everything to before they have shared too much. They may prefer to go to HR, for example.
- Listen without judgment or presumption

The Don'ts

- Ask them why they haven't left or why they stayed
- Tell them to leave
- Make assumptions about their situation
- Presume that you know how they feel
- Make judgments; even if you have been through abuse yourself, you do not know their situation

Obviously these are not exhaustive lists, but these reminders will facilitate empathetic communication, which is a good start, because they will help the person disclosing feel safe and understood. This in turn will help to minimise the chance of further trauma.

Believe me when I say that disclosing domestic violence is never easy, especially in the workplace. If the disclosure doesn't go well, the person disclosing could feel unsafe and decide it was wrong to speak up. It may take months or even years for them to speak up again.

Remember to check your unconscious bias when talking about domestic violence in the workplace. Obviously being unconscious it is hard for us to recognise in ourselves. But we can challenge our beliefs and thoughts especially when they are not helping or adding anything positive to the situation.

A special note: why you shouldn't tell the abused person to 'just leave' the situation

When someone discloses that they are in an abusive relationship, it is tempting to tell them to leave. On the surface, it makes sense. They are being abused, and their life could even be in danger.

I realise that this might seem the most logical course of action. But there are many reasons why somebody might not leave. You also must understand that leaving is the most dangerous time in an abusive relationship.

A psychologically abusive situation can become violent when the abused partner announces that they want to leave. This is because domestic violence is about power and control. When a partner threatens to leave, it means a loss of that power and control, which can escalate abusive behaviours. An abusive relationship previously without physical abuse can quickly become physically dangerous.

In fact, the false sense of security that comes with the lack of physical violence can be detrimental to the safety of the person leaving. Knowing an abusive partner has been violent in the past means the victim is very cautious, and the precautions needed are often in place.

When I was with my abusive partner there were too many physically violent incidents to count. This violence meant I knew what he was capable of physically, and that my life might be in danger and I would need to be very cautious about leaving and staying safe. I refused to meet him or have any unsupervised access to him because of this. I took every precaution I could. It is the reason I stayed in a refuge and applied for an Apprehended Violence Order.

Those who are in an abusive relationship that does not include physical violence often have a false sense of security that the abuse will never escalate to physical assault, which is not the case. The police see this lack of physical violence in an otherwise abusive relationship as a zero percent indicator that there will be no escalation to physical violence, up to and including homicide when the abused partner tries to leave the relationship.

It is important to gather as much information as you can, but at the same time, it is important to advise the abused person about the threat to their physical safety. Keep in mind that family members, children and pets could also be in danger.

A safety and exit plan is needed, of course. If the abused person can find a safe time to leave, then that is the right time to leave. But the safe time to leave may not be at the same time that they are disclosing their situation.

I had to wait four days after deciding to leave for my partner to go away on business, before it was safe for me to move to a domestic violence shelter with my children. This delay was dangerous, but not as dangerous as getting caught trying to leave.

In addition, there is a shortage of places in refuges, and the abused person may not have an alternative place to go. Staying with family often is not an option, as it is too easy for the abuser to find them. This puts both the victim and their family in danger.

This is a time to help them understand the gravity of their situation. They will have normalised the abuse as it escalated, and they may not be aware of how destructive and serious their situation is.

Be gentle, and don't be judgmental or demand a certain course of action — however much it seems to make sense to you for their safety. Their abuser is already making demands on them. The most important thing is to keep the lines of communication open and to build trust. This will help them work out a plan and feel supported when they leave.

You cannot rescue them, but you can inform and support them. Trust them when they say it is not safe to leave at the moment, but keep the lines of communication open. They have spent the entirety of their relationship confused and scared, so it is important they have someone with whom they have an open line of communication.

It is equally important you know your boundaries as you lead them through the stormy waters — for both their sake and yours. The stories they tell may be difficult to hear; therefore, it is important that you yourself are supported as you support them.

Communicating with co-workers that you suspect may be in an abusive relationship

When talking to someone that your suspect is in an abusive relationship, remember: don't presume, and don't judge. Start a conversation and let them know that you are worried about them. If you are in a position of authority over them, reassure them this is not a conversation about the quality of their work; if you are not clear on your intent it could add to their stress.

Invite them to share with you any concerns they may have. If they are reluctant, do not push them, as they are used to being controlled and may see you as another person in control of their life. It is important that they are in charge of their decisions. If they are really resistant to discussing things, respect their wishes.

Ask them if you can share with them a list of people who it is safe to talk to within your workplace (if it has such a list) along with external resources – it may be they do not want to share with you for a number of reasons. But you will have opened the door for them to reach out for help. Make sure they have the details of your Employee Assist Program if you company has one. Whether they use it or not is out of your hands.

Remember that those in abusive relationships often don't recognise that they are in one. Tell them why you are concerned, so they can understand why you are worried. This could help them start to comprehend what is happening to them.

It may not seem like you are doing enough, but this may be the first conversation they have had and may open them up to the idea that their relationship may indeed be abusive.

Tread gently and keep the lines of communication open. If you are concerned for their safety, let them know and suggest a safety plan.

A note on using the term victim

I am happy to use the word 'victim' to describe myself in my prior life when I lived with abuse.

Describing myself as someone who was a victim to me seems fitting, given that I spent almost four decades of my life being victimised. I do not see admitting that as a weakness. In fact, I see it as just the opposite. For decades, I was abused, degraded and treated less than human, and I am here: strong, independent and proud of who I am.

If I refuse to see myself as a victim then, for me, I am minimising my experiences, including the strength it took to survive—to literally find the will to breathe in and out. Sometimes getting through the next minute seemed like an insurmountable mountain. I am proud that I found the strength to climb those mountains, one at a time.

I am grateful that I found the courage to reach out for help. The world had not been kind to me, and being vulnerable and trusting took more courage than I believed I had. I am so thankful for the crisis workers, counsellors, social workers and doctors who helped me as I tentatively entered a world free of abuse—a world so alien to me that it scared me more than living with abuse. Without these outstanding people, I would not have been able to heal.

I am a survivor. This is something that defines my sense of self. I found the courage day by day, hour by hour and minute by minute to keep going. Understanding the magnitude of what I had been through was possibly worse than going through the abuse in the first place.

I was victimised, which made me a victim. I survived, which makes me a survivor. It takes great inner strength to survive being victimised, and acknowledging my victimhood makes it possible to take pride in that strength.

Not everyone who has been through abuse feels the same way about the word victim. For those who have experienced abuse and survived, it is for them to decide how they would like others to refer to their experiences. It is up to them to define it, no one else.

It is important to see the person, not just their circumstance. This is a stage in their life and it does not define them as a person. So, when talking to someone who has been or is living with abuse, remember to see the individual—not simply a 'victim' of domestic violence.

When I left my relationship, I went straight to a shelter. I had two bags of clothes, one bag of toys, $33 and more debt than I care to mention. It was daunting, and I truly believed I did not have what it would take to rebuild my life. I would need all the resilience I had.

I had spent my whole life living with abuse. I was worn down. I was broken. But what I didn't realise was that the very skills that made it possible for me to stay in an abusive relationship would be the same attributes I needed to change the trajectory of my life.

I left my ex five times before I finally made it stick. Each time I learned something, such as to forget the things that don't matter and focus on legal documents and some items of sentimental value. The day I left, I couldn't find my jewellery, some of which was family heirlooms. This broke my heart, but it was the right time to leave.

Luckily, my nan had a saying that I heard all through my childhood: 'If things become more important than people, it is a sorry state of affairs'. So, I let go of things and held on to the memories associated with them.

Every time I went back to my partner, there were promises of a new start, apologies and assurances that it would never ever happen again. But the opposite was true; each time I returned the bar was lowered, and he would treat me even worse than before.

It took enormous strength and resilience to survive that relationship. I needed my wits about me all the time. I wonder how I would have coped day-to-day without that resilience. Maybe I would have left sooner. I will never know.

What I do know is that the resilience I had learned would be needed every day for years after I left. The strength that had helped me to tolerate the most despicable behaviour could now be used to heal and rebuild my life from the ground up.

I had to teach myself self-worth and self-care. I had neither. I believed the horrible things I had been told. I had no idea just how low I had become. I was a shell of a person.

If someone discloses that they are or were in an abusive relationship, think about what it took for them to survive and recognise the trust they are placing in you, by sharing their story with you. If they tell you they are still in an abusive relationship, don't simply feel sorry for them. They are reaching out for help.

They have the strength and resilience inside to cope. But they need help and support. Dealing with a violent relationship is scary and dangerous.

CHAPTER TEN
Final Thoughts

Having lived with abuse for nearly four decades, I know firsthand the devastating impact it has on someone's life. My own life was left in ruins financially, emotionally, psychologically and physically. Climbing out of the debris and understanding not only what had been done to me, but the impact it had, took a decade of hard work and dedication to heal.

This lived and learned experience, along with the experience gained working with business and Government for the last three years since setting up my business, has given me a great deal of insight into what can be done.

Domestic family violence has literally been the focus of my life for five decades, and I have gained knowledge on what works and what doesn't. I often describe the language of abuse as my first language, and I have been learning the language of healthy relationship and friendships for the last twelve years.

I hope to continue to learn how workplaces can best support both employees and customers, along with other contributions that I and the organisations I work with can make to positive change on the issue of domestic violence.

I have hope that change will come because of the ground gained in recognising and dealing with mental health in the workplace. Companies now even have mental health first aiders. Struggling with mental health used to be something employees would try hard to hide from employers. Now, many companies actively encourage employees to speak up. I see this trend starting with domestic violence.

Employees will disclose when they feel their workplace is safe, which means that we must create an environment which is conducive to disclosure. This means tackling workplace bullying and harassment at all levels. Sexist and demeaning behaviour has no place in a healthy workplace.

When we think of how diverse our workplaces are, we must think about how the LGBTI, culturally-diverse, indigenous and disabled communities are included in our training and the broader conversation about domestic violence. Although the support they need may be different, the impact domestic violence has on their lives is not.

One of the things that troubles me most when I go into companies is the resistance to move forward for fear of getting it wrong. Of course we need to proceed with informed caution. As the Hippocratic Oath for doctors states, 'First, Do No Harm', but we do need to progress.

We are going to make mistakes, and this truth feels awful when dealing with domestic violence, but there will be no progress without mistakes. What we need to do is make sure that we learn from these mistakes and share our learnings, because making the same mistake over and over is irresponsible and the cost is too high.

APPENDIX

Seeking Help and Key Statistics

Note: these statistics are correct at the time of publication.

There are difficulties in accurately recording domestic violence statistics due to factors including social stigma, minimisation and a lack of disclosure. There is also often a lack of data available for some marginalised groups, including the LGBTI community, Indigenous comminites, culturally and linguistically diverse communities (CALD) and the disabled community among others. Different countries have different statistics available.

If some statistics are not included in this section, is because they were not available. This is in no way a reflection of the importance I place on these areas of domestic violence. Domestic violence is unacceptable, no matter who is the victim and who is perpetrator. This is one of my core beliefs.

If you are in a foreign country and need assistance, remember your local embassy may be of assistance.

Australia

**Important numbers
By state:**

Australian Capital Territory
Domestic Violence Crisis Service ACT
www.dvcs.org.au
Phone: (02) 6280 0900

New South Wales
Domestic Violence Line
www.domesticviolence.nsw.gov.au/home
Phone: 1800 65 64 63

Northern Territory
Dawn House
Phone: (08) 8945 1388

Queensland
DV Connect
www.dvconnect.org
Phone: 1800 811 811

South Australia
Domestic Violence Crisis Service
Phone: 1300 782 200

Tasmania
Family Violence Response Referral line
www.safeathome.tas.gov.au/about_us
Phone: 1800 633 937

Victoria
Safe Steps Family Violence Response Centre
www.safesteps.org.au
Phone: 1800 015 188

Western Australia
Women's Domestic Violence Helpline
Phone: 1800 007 339 or (08) 9223 1188

National
Domestic violence and sexual assault helpline: **1800 RESPECT (1800 737 732)**
Lifeline: mental health helpline: **13 11 14**
Suicide call-back service: **1300 659 467**

Key Statistics
- **One in three women** have experienced physical and/or sexual violence perpetrated by someone

known to them[1]
- **One in five women** over 18 have been stalked during their lifetime[2]
- **One in five women** experience harassment within the workplace[3]
- Over twelve months, an average of **one woman each week is killed** by a partner or former partner[4]
- Domestic and family violence is the **principal cause of homelessness for women and children**[5]
- **One in twenty men** has experienced violence from a partner since the age of 15[6]
- A national survey on violence against women suggested that **sexual violence against**

1 Australian Bureau of Statistics (2013) *Personal Safety, Australia, 2012,* cat. no 4906.0 Retrieved from White Ribbon Australia, 2014

2 Australian Bureau of Statistics (2013) *Personal Safety, Australia, 2012,* cat. no 4906.0 Retrieved from White Ribbon Australia, 2014

3 Australian Human Rights Commission (2008). *Sexual Harassment Guide.* Retrieved from White Ribbon Australia, 2014

4 Chan. A. and Payne. K (2013) Homicide in Australia: 2008-09 to 2009-10, *National Homicide Monitoring Program annual report.* Canberra, Australia, Australian Institute of Criminology. Retrieved from White Ribbon Australia, 2014

5 Australian Institute of Health and Welfare (2013) *Specialist homelessness services 2012-2013,* cat. no HOU 273 Retrieved from White Ribbon Australia, 2014

6 Australian Bureau of Statistics (2013)

Indigenous women was three times as common as against non-Indigenous women[7]

- **CALD women are as likely to be at risk** as non-CALD women[8]

The financial implications[9]

- Violence against women by a partner is estimated to cost **$12.6 billion** ($9.6 billion USD)
- The costs of pain, suffering and premature mortality now estimated to total more than **$10.4 billion** a year ($7.9 billion USD)
- **$7.8 billion** a year is spent on the criminal justice system and programs delivering health services and social welfare to domestic violence survivors ($5.9 billion USD)
- Lost productivity is anticipated to cost **$2.1 billion** to the economy ($1.6 billion USD)

7   Mouzos & Makkai, ibid.

8   Mouzos & Makkai, ibid.

9   https://www.pwc.com.au/pdf/a-high-price-to-pay.pdf

Canada

Important numbers

Ontario
Assaulted Women's Helpline: Provides anonymous and confidential crisis counseling, informational and emotional support to women. (Toronto, ON)
Toll Free: 1-866-863-0511
Toll Free TTY: 1-866-863-7868
Mental Health Crisis Line: A 24/7 helpline to assist people experiencing a mental health problem or crisis. (Ottawa, ON)
Telephone: 613-722-6914
Toll Free: 1-866-996-0991

British Columbia
Battered Women's Support Services: Provides education, advocacy and support services to assist women. (Vancouver, BC)
Crisis line: 604-687-1867
Toll Free: 1-855-687-1868

Alberta
Family Violence Info Line: 24/7 helpline in over 170 languages to provide support and advice for people experiencing family violence.
Telephone: 780-310-1818

Saskatchewan
La Ronge 24-Hour Crisis Line: General crisis line for men and women in crisis in La Ronge, Saskatchewan. (La Ronge, SK)
Crisis Line: 306-425-4090

Manitoba
Toll-Free Province Wide Domestic Abuse Crisis Line (24 hours): General crisis line for people experiencing domestic violence and abuse in the province of Manitoba.
Toll Free: 1-877-977-0007

Northwest Territories
NWT Help Line: General helpline there to provide support to those in crisis.
Telephone: 1-800-661-0844

Nunavut
Nunavut Kamatsiaqtut Help Line: Provides anonymous and confidential counseling for northerners in crisis.

Telephone: 867-979-3333
Toll Free: 1-800-265-3333

Quebec
Domestic Violence Hotline: Provides anonymous and confidential domestic violence services via telephone or email. (Montreal, QC)
Telephone: 514-873-9010
Toll free: 1-800-363-9010

Newfoundland
Hope Haven Transition House Crisis Line:
Provides confidential and safe emergency shelter to women and children who are experiencing violence and abuse. 24-hour crisis line offers information, emergency planning and emotional support.
(Labrador City, NL)
Crisis Line: (709) 944-6900
Toll Free: 1-888-332-0000

Nova Scotia
Helpline: General helpline for people experiencing crisis in Nova Scotia.
Toll Free: 1-877-521-1188
TTY: 1-855-443-2660

For mental health and suicide hotlines, search online for provision in your local area.

Key statistics

- **Half of all women** in Canada have experienced at least one incident of physical or sexual violence since the age of 16[10]
- **3% of women report being a victim of stalking**, double the rate for men[11]
- **43% of Canadian women** have experienced harassment at work[12]
- On any given night in Canada, **3,491 women and their 2,724 children sleep in shelters** because it isn't safe at home.[13] On any given night, about **300 women and children are turned away** because shelters are already full[14].
- Approximately **every six days, a woman in Canada is killed** by her intimate partner[15]
- Women who identify as **lesbian or bisexual were three to four times** more likely than

---

10 The Violence Against Women Survey, Statistics Canada, 1993.

11 Statistics Canada. (2013). Measuring violence against women: Statistical trends. Ottawa, ON: Minister of Industry. Pg. 33.

12 http://angusreid.org/wp-content/uploads/2014/12/2014.12.05-Sexual-Harassment-at-work.pdf accessed 08/06/2018

13 Shelters for Abused Women in Canada, 2014, Statistics Canada, Available here. Out of the 4,476 women and 3,493 children staying in shelters on the snapshot date of April 16, 2014, 78% (or 3,491 women and 2,742 children) were there primarily because of abuse.

14 Shelters for abused Women in Canada, 2014, Statistics Canada.

15 Homicide in Canada, 2014, Statistics Canada, Table 6.

heterosexual women to report experiencing
spousal violence[16]

- **Aboriginal women (First Nations, Inuit and Métis) are 2.5 times more likely** to experience spousal violence than non-Aboriginal women[17]
- Canadian men are half as likely as women to experience domestic violence[18]
- Women living with **physical and cognitive impairments experience violence two to three times** more often than women living without impairments[19]

The financial implications[20]

- The total economic impact of spousal violence per year is **$7.4 billion,** ($5.7 billion USD) amounting to **$220** ($170 USD) per Canadian
- The justice system bears **$545.2 million** ($420 million USD) of the total economic impact

16 Family Violence in Canada: a Statistical Profile, 2014, Statistics Canada, p. 14.

17 Violence Against Women in Canada Fact Sheet, Status of Women Canada (2013), p. 2.

18 Family Violence in Canada, A Statistical Profile, 2013.

19 Violence Against Women with DisAbilities and Deaf Women: an overview (2103), By Odette, F. and Rajan, D., p. 3.

20 An Estimation of the Economic Impact of Spousal Violence in Canada, 2009 http://www.justice.gc.ca/eng/rp-pr/cj-jp/fv-vf/rr12_7/p0.html#sum accessed 08/06/2018

- **$5.5 billion** ($4.2 billion USD) of the economic impact of spousal violence is in the form of intangible costs to both victims (pain and suffering and loss of life) and family members (loss of affection and enjoyment)
- **$0.1 billion** ($0.78 billion USD) is borne by the private sector through lost output, lost productivity due to tardiness and distraction, and associated administration costs

Ireland

Important numbers

Ireland Women's Aid for domestic abuse and sexual assault: 1800 341 900
Aware (Depression & Bi-Polar Disorder) Tel: 1800 80 48 48
Samaritans: 087 2 60 90 90
National Suicide Helpline (Pieta House) 1800 247 247

Key Statistics
- **1 in 5 women** in Ireland who have been in a relationship have been abused by a current or former partner[21]
- 12% of Irish respondents in the FRA study had experienced stalking (including cyber stalking)
- Since 1996, **216 women have died violently** in the Republic of Ireland[22]

---

21 O,Connor, M, & Kelleher Associates, Making the Links, Women's Aid, 1995.
22 Women's Aid Femicide Watch 2017

- In 2003, **26% of women** who presented as homeless to the Irish Homeless Persons Unit had become homeless as a result of domestic violence[23]
- **1 in 7 women** in Ireland compared to **1 in 17 men** experience severe domestic violence[24]
- **37% of women** accessing refuge identified themselves as Travellers, **6% as Black**, and **2% as Asian**[25]

The financial implications

- The estimated economic cost of domestic violence to the Irish economy is **€2.2billion** ($2.6 billion USD) a year[26]

---

23 O'Connor & Wilson, Safe Home, Sonas Housing Association Model of Supported Transitional Housing, 2004.

24 Domestic Abuse of Women and Men in Ireland: Report on the National Study of Domestic Abuse, National Crime Council and ERSI, 2005.

25 It is important not to draw conclusions about levels or severity of domestic violence amongst particular minority ethnic communities given some appear 'over-represented' in refuge provision. Instead it shows that minority women face additional barriers to obtaining long-term safety and lack other possible options than emergency accommodation. [SAFE Ireland (2009) Safety & Change: A national study of support needs and outcomes for women accessing refuge provision in Ireland]

26 Ahern, TD, Dermot, Minister for Justice, speaking at the International Conference on Domestic Violence, Waterford, May 2008, quoted in 'Domestic Violence costs the country €2.2bn', The Irish Examiner, 30.5.08.

- SAFE Ireland is currently undertaking a "Cost of Violence Study in Ireland" in partnership with Dr Nata Duvvury in NUI Galway

New Zealand

Important Numbers

**Are You Okay (family violence helpline):
0800 456 450**
**Shine (confidential domestic abuse helpline):
0508 744 633**
Rape Crisis: 0800 883 300
**Lifeline (mental health support: 0800 543 354
(0800 LIFELINE) or free text 4357 (HELP)**
**Suicide Crisis Helpline: 0508 828 865 (0508
TAUTOKO)**

Key Statistics
- **1 in 3 women** are affected by domestic violence in New Zealand[27]
- **13 women a year** are murdered by a partner or former partner[28]

---

27 (1) Family Violence Death Review Committee. (2014). Fourth Annual Report: January 2013 to December 2013. Wellington, Health Quality and Safety Commission. Retrieved June 2014 from http://www.hqsc.govt.nz/our-programmes/mrc/fvdrc/publications-and-resources/publication/1600/

28 (1) Family Violence Death Review Committee. (2014). Fourth Annual

- **Disabled women are twice as likely** to be victims of violence or abuse compared to other women[29]

- **Maori women twice as likely** to experience domestic violence[30]

The financial implications[31]

- **$377 million** ($265 million USD) goes towards the annual health costs of domestic violence
- **$1 billion** ($0.7 billion USD) is lost to the economy in productivity
- **$840 million** ($591 million USD) is spent on victim and survivor support each year

---

Report: January 2013 to December 2013. Wellington, Health Quality and Safety Commission. Retrieved June 2014 from http://www.hqsc.govt.nz/our-programmes/mrc/fvdrc/publications-and-resources/publication/1600/

29 (6) Brownridge, D. (2006). Partner violence against women with disabilities: Prevalence, risk and explanations. Violence against women 12(9), 805-822.
http://web.usu.edu/saavi/docs/partner_violence_women_with_disabilities_805.pdf

30 http://women.govt.nz/sites/public_files/Wahine%20Maori%20wahine%20ora%20wahine%20kaha.pdf

31 https://www.tvnz.co.nz/one-news/new-zealand/domestic-violence-could-cost-nz-80b-over-next-ten-years-new-report-6126548

United Kingdom

Important numbers

24-hour National Domestic Violence Freephone Helpline: 0808 2000 247
Northern Ireland Domestic Violence Helpline: 0808 802 1414
Rape Crisis national freephone helpline: 0808 802 9999
Northern Ireland: 0808 802 1414
Centrepoint Young and Homeless helpline 0808 800 0661
Shelter — free housing advice helpline 0808 800 4444

Key Statistics
- Domestic abuse affects **1 in 4 women**[32]
- **1 in 5 women** will experience stalking in their adult life[33]

---

32 Office for National Statistics (2016) Focus on Violent Crime and Sexual Offences, 2014/15.

33 Homicides, Firearm offences and intimate violence 2009/10; Supplementary Volume 2 to Crime in England and Wales 2009/10 2nd Edition. Home Office Statistical Bulletin 01/11.

- **More than half of women** have suffered sexual harassment in the workplace[34]
- **2 women a week are killed** by a partner or former partner[35]
- Domestic violence is the **single most quoted reason for becoming homeless**[36]
- **1 in 6 men** will be affected by domestic abuse in their lifetime[37]
- **Women with a disability** experience domestic violence at **double the rate** of women without a disability[38]
- **One in four lesbian and bi women** have experienced domestic abuse in a relationship.[39] **Almost half (49%) of all gay and bi men** have experienced at least one incident of domestic abuse

---

34 Researchers from the Trades Union Congress and the Everyday Sexism Project found that 52% of women had experienced unwanted behaviour at work including groping, sexual advances and inappropriate jokes. Among women and girls aged 16-24, the proportion reporting sexual harassment rose to 63%.

35 Office for National Statistics (2016) Compendium – Homicide (average taken over 10 years).

36 Shelter, 2002

37 http://www.lwa.org.uk/understanding-abuse/statistics.htm

38 http://www.domesticviolencelondon.nhs.uk/1-what-is-domestic-violence-/21-domestic-abuse-perpetrated-against-people-with-disabilities.html

39 https://www.stonewall.org.uk/help-advice/criminal-law/domestic-violence

from a family member or partner since the age of 16.[40]

The financial implications[41]

- The cost of domestic violence to the British economy is estimated at **£23 billion per annum** ($38 billion USD)
- The Home Office estimates that each domestic abuse murder costs the country just over **£1 million** ($1.3 million USD)
- British employers lose an estimated **£2.7 billion** ($3.6 billion USD) per year as a result of domestic violence

---

40 https://www.stonewall.org.uk/help-advice/criminal-law/domestic-violence

41 http://www.lwa.org.uk/understanding-abuse/statistics.htm

United States

Important numbers

> **Domestic Violence helpline: CALL 24/7/365**
> **1-800-799-SAFE (7233)**
> **1-800-787-3224 (TTY for Deaf/Hard of Hearing)**
> **Mental Health helpline RAINN: 800-656-HOPE (4673)**
> **Suicide Prevention helpline: 1-800-273-8255**

Key Statistics
- **1 in 3 women** and **1 in 4 men** have been victims of physical violence by an intimate partner within their lifetime[42]
- **1 in 7 women** have been stalked by an intimate partner during their lifetime[43]
- **1 in 4 women** experience harassment in their

---

42 National Intimate Partner and Sexual Violence Survey 2010 Summary Report.

43 National Intimate Partner and Sexual Violence Survey 2010 Summary Report.

workplace[44]

- **3 women per day are murdered** by a partner or former partner[45]
- The presence of a gun in a domestic violence situation increases the risk of homicide by **500%**[46]
- **44% of percent of lesbian women and 61% of bisexual women** experienced rape, physical violence, and/or stalking by an intimate partner in their lifetime[47]
- **26% percent of gay men and 37% of bisexual men** – compared to 29% of heterosexual men – experienced rape, physical violence, and/or stalking by an intimate partner at some point in their lifetime[48]

---

44 https://www.cosmopolitan.com/career/news/a36453/cosmopolitan-sexual-harassment-survey/

45 When Men Murder Women: An Analysis of 2015 Homicide Data, Violence Policy Center.

46 Campbell JC, Webster D, Koziol-McLain J, et al. Risk Factors for Femicide in Abusive Relationships: Results From a Multisite Case Control Study. *American Journal of Public Health.* 2003;93(7):1089-1097.

47 National Intimate Partner and Sexual Violence Survey, 2010 Summary Report. National Center for Injury Prevention and Control, Division of Violence Prevention, Atlanta, GA, and Control of the Centers for Disease Control and Prevention.

48 National Intimate Partner and Sexual Violence Survey, 2010 Summary Report. National Center for Injury Prevention and Control, Division of Violence Prevention, Atlanta, GA, and Control of the Centers for Disease Control and Prevention.

- **Approximately 50% of all women who are homeless** report that domestic violence was the immediate cause of their homelessness[49]
- Approximately **4 out of every 10 Black women** (43.7%), **4 out of every 10 American Indian** or Alaska Native women (46.0%), and **1 in 2 multiracial women** (53.8%) have been the victim of rape, physical violence, and/or stalking by an intimate partner in their lifetime[50]

The financial implications[51]

- Victims of intimate partner violence lose a total of **8 million days of paid work** each year
- The cost of intimate partner violence exceeds **$8.3 billion** per year
- Between **21-60% of victims of intimate partner violence lose their jobs** due to reasons stemming from the abuse

---

49 *"Pressing Issues Facing Families Who Are Homeless." The National Center on Family Homelessness. (2013)*

50 *National Intimate Partner and Sexual Violence Survey, 2010 Summary Report. National Center for Injury Prevention and Control, Division of Violence Prevention, Atlanta, GA, and Control of the Centers for Disease Control and Prevention.*

51 Rothman, E. F., Hathaway, J., Stidsen, A., & de Vries, H. F. (2007). How employment helps female victims of intimate partner violence: A qualitative study. *Journal of Occupational Health Psychology, 12*(2), 136-143.

Further Reading and Resources

The following is a list of books that helped me understand domestic violence and books that helped me heal. Some are suitable for the workplace; others are aimed at those going through domestic violence or healing and trying to make sense of what happened to them.

This is my personal list, they may not resonate with you, but there are many great books, resources and articles out there. The more we read, the more we understand. This is a great place to start the conversation.

The Verbally Abusive Relationship – Patricia Evans

Why does he do that? – Lundy Bancroft

The BRAIN *the CHANGES ITSELF* – Norman Doidge M.D.

Reinventing Your Life – Jeffrey E. Young, Ph.D, Janet Klosko, Ph.D

I Can't Get Over It – Aphrodite Marsakia, Ph.D

Feel the Fear and Do it Anyway – Susan Jeffers

You Can Heal Your Life – Louise L. Hay

Index

A

abuser: xxii, 6, 10, 12-13, 15, 18, 20, 22, 24-27, 33, 39-42, 46, 52-63, 65-71, 78-79, 102-103, 114, 119, 134, 141, 143-144, 148, 160, 197

abusive partner: xx, 6, 17, 24, 32, 41, 57, 78, 102-103, 112, 115, 126, 130, 135-136, 149-151, 158, 197

abusive relationship: x, xx, 3, 5, 9, 11, 16-17, 19, 32-33, 40, 49, 51-53, 57, 61, 66, 73, 79, 81-83, 85, 90, 100, 110, 113, 123, 130-132, 138, 141, 149-155, 158-159, 161, 165-166, 195, 197

alcohol: 13-14, 197

B

bullied: 45-46, 136, 197

bullies: 45, 86-87, 197

C

child abuse: 3, 8, 90, 197

childhood domestic violence: 8, 197

code of silence: 95-96, 99, 197

communication: xx, 3, 53, 115, 136, 138, 150-151, 156-157, 160, 162, 197

confidential: 27, 102-103, 177-179, 186, 197

confidentiality: 113, 197

corporate social responsibility: 89, 91, 197

corporate training: 91, 197

cost: xxix, 94-95, 97-98, 111, 120, 131, 169, 176, 184-185,

190, 193, 197

co-worker: x, 11, 13, 72-73, 123, 133, 135, 149, 153, 198

co-workers: xx, xxi, 5, 15, 17, 26, 32, 52, 64, 72, 79-80, 82, 87, 96-99, 125, 128, 139, 161, 198

crazy-making: 35, 38, 41, 64, 119, 126, 198

culturally-diverse communities: 198

customer: 110, 148, 198

cyber security: 27, 102, 198

cycle of violence: 47-49, 198

D

disabled communities: 168, 198

disclosure: 5, 77, 83, 104, 109-110, 147, 153-155, 157, 168, 171, 198

domestic abuse: xx, xxix, 5, 7, 9, 58, 84, 94-96, 114, 151, 153, 178, 183-184, 186, 188-190, 198

domestic family violence – DFV: 7, 198

domestic violence: i, ii, iii, vii, ix, x, xvii, xix, xx, xxi, xxii, xxiii, xxviii, xxix, 1, 3, 5-9, 11-12, 14, 21, 27-29, 34, 48, 51, 59, 73, 77-87, 89-94, 96-99, 102, 105-108, 111, 113-114, 116-120, 130, 147-150, 152, 154, 156-158, 160, 164, 168-169, 171, 173-174, 176, 178-179, 181, 184, 186-193, 195, 197-199, 201

domestic violence and emotional health: 83, 198

domestic violence and mental health: 83, 119, 198

domestic violence – DV: 7, 198

E

emotional and psychological abuse: 9, 16, 150, 198

emotional or psychological abuse: 8, 198

entrapment: 34, 48, 53, 55-56, 58, 72, 198

explosion: 48, 50, 63-64, 67, 70, 72, 198

F

family abuse: 7, 109, 198

financial abuse: ii, 7-9, 20-23, 153, 199

financial security: 21, 78, 81, 83-84, 116, 199

G

gaslighting: 40-41, 119, 199

grooming: 32-34, 45, 64-65, 68, 199

guilt: 59, 67, 144, 199

H

hacking: 25, 27, 199

harassment: 25, 32, 92, 168, 175, 180, 189, 191, 199, 201

helplessness: 38-39, 70-71, 131, 199

I

image-based abuse: 8, 10, 199

impersonation: 26, 199

indigenous: 29, 168, 171, 176, 199

indigenous employees: 29, 199

intimate partner violence – IPV: 7, 199

intimate terrorism: 7, 199

isolate: 26, 41, 82, 128, 199

isolating: 5, 18, 41, 126-127, 136, 199

isolation: 9, 17, 41, 43, 50, 54, 58, 66, 97, 125, 135, 199

J

joint finances: 153-154, 199

justification: 65, 199

L

learned helplessness: 39, 71, 131, 199

M

managers: xix, xx, 72, 95, 98, 112-113, 152, 199

minimisation: 66, 171, 199

monitoring and stalking: 25, 199

P

paid domestic violence leave: 114, 117, 199

paid leave: 112-113, 115-117, 199

partner abuse: 7, 199

patterns of behaviour: 52, 72, 138, 199

perpetrator: 8, 84, 86, 171, 200

perpetrators: xxii, 24, 32, 85-87, 117, 200

physical abuse: 8-9, 11-13, 52, 66, 68, 135, 158, 200

physical violence: 7, 9, 13, 15, 52, 64, 158-159, 191-193, 200

policies and procedures: xix, 77, 149, 200

policies, procedures and guidelines: 106, 200

power and control: 7, 13, 15, 25-27, 29, 32, 39, 85, 108, 158, 200

pre-groomed: 34, 200

productivity: 72, 91-92, 94-95, 98, 101, 105, 116, 119-120, 142-143, 176, 182, 187, 200

psychologically and emotionally: 11, 200

psychologically and emotionally abused: 11, 200

pursuit phase: 69, 71, 200

R

recruitment costs: 91, 97, 200

reduced absenteeism: 99, 200

remorse phase, or the 'pretending to be sorry' phase: 65, 200

reproductive abuse: 16, 200

revenge porn: 10, 200

S

safety plan: 112, 117-118, 132, 148, 162, 200

sexual abuse: 8, 10, 14, 200

sexual assault: 10, 14-15, 174, 183, 200

social abuse: 9, 200

spiritual: 8, 10, 28, 200

spiritual and cultural: 10, 28, 200

spiritual and cultural abuse: 28, 200

stalked: 24, 175, 191, 200

stalking: 10, 25, 180, 183, 188, 192-193, 199-200

stand-over: 60, 62, 72, 200

T

team cohesion: 94, 100, 200

technologically facilitated abuse: 8, 10, 24-25, 27, 102, 200-201 technologically facilitated abuse — TFA: 8, 201

tension build-up phase: 55, 60, 201

the LGTBI community: 28, 201

threats: 9, 17-18, 26, 70-71, 132, 201

tracking devices: 10, 25-26, 115, 201

training: xvii, xxix, 73, 78-79, 81, 83-84, 90-96, 98, 106, 111, 113-114, 116, 120, 149, 151-152, 168, 197, 201

types of abuse: 8, 11, 83, 119, 201

V

verbal abuse: 8-9, 19-20, 201

victim: xxii, xxiii, 5-6, 9-10, 18, 25, 29, 40, 43, 46, 52, 54, 57, 69-70, 79, 81, 84-85, 113, 116-117, 119, 126, 129-130, 143, 148, 151, 153, 158, 160, 162-164, 171, 180, 187, 193, 201

victim-blaming: 43, 201

victims: i, xxi, xxii, 5, 24, 29, 32, 52, 58, 78, 85, 93, 96, 100, 110, 113, 115-116, 120, 152-153, 182, 187, 191, 193, 201

W

workplace: i, v, x, xvii, xix, xx, 32, 59, 75, 77-79, 81-82, 84-87, 91-93, 95, 106, 111, 119-120, 128, 136, 147, 154-155, 157, 161, 168, 175, 189, 192, 195, 201

workplace bullying and harassment: 32, 168, 201

workplace domestic violence policy: 92, 201

workplace-specific behaviours: 141, 201

Notes

Notes

Notes

Notes

Notes